HOW TO DO BUSINESS IN MEXICO

GLENN REED
&
ROGER GRAY

HOW TO DO BUSINESS IN MEXICO

*Your Essential
and Up-to-date
Guide for Success*

UNIVERSITY OF TEXAS PRESS

AUSTIN

Requests for permission to reproduce material from this work should
be sent to Permissions, University of Texas Press, P.O. Box 7819,
Austin, TX 78713-7819.

♾ The paper used in this publication meets the minimum requirements of American National Standard for Information Sciences—
Permanence of Paper for Printed Library Materials, ANSI Z39.48-1984.

LIBRARY OF CONGRESS CATALOGING-IN-PUBLICATION DATA

Reed, Glenn, 1930–
    How to do business in Mexico : your essential and up-to-date guide
for success / by Glenn Reed and Roger Gray.
        p.   cm.
    Includes index.
    ISBN 0-292-77079-0 (hardcover : alk. paper). —
    ISBN 0-292-77080-4 (pbk. : alk. paper)
        1. Mexico—Commerce—Handbooks, manuals, etc.   2. Mexico—
Description and travel.   I. Gray, Roger, 1953–   .   II. Title.
HF3237.R44   1997
658.8'48'0972—dc20   96-22353

CONTENTS

PREFACE

When we began writing this book, the issue of free trade with Mexico was being hotly debated in both houses of Congress. The world's spotlight was on Mexican president Carlos Salinas de Gortari, and many media pundits predicted that NAFTA would fail miserably.

The pundits were wrong: NAFTA passed decisively. However, former president Salinas, then the man of the hour, has fallen from grace as a result of suspicions aroused by a series of political assassinations and the precipitous collapse of the peso within days of his leaving office.

Whatever the outcome of any investigation regarding Salinas' linkage to the monetary crisis and the political mayhem preceding the election of his successor, Ernesto Zedillo, his monumental restructuring of Mexico transformed the face and fiber of the country more than any action since the revolution of 1910.

Mexico's markets are open, and trade is proceeding at a blistering pace in spite of the economic downturn.

While we could not predict the political and economic events that occurred after the passage of NAFTA, we were accurate in our evaluation of the opportunities that this re-markable change in Mexico's trade policies would unleash.

Now that NAFTA is changing the face of trade in North America, there is a very real need for a single source of hard information and social/cultural guidelines for U.S. citizens doing business in Mexico.

Few places on earth have two neighboring cultures as di-verse as those of Mexico and the United States. Because of Mexico's longstanding insularity, communications between the countries atrophied. In order to realize the new trade op-portunities, we first need to understand how to deal with each other socially.

Our decades of real business experience in Mexico have provided us with a unique insight into this crucial market and the forces that spell the difference between success and failure. This book combines our ongoing experience in this rapidly changing market with a hard-earned understanding of the underlying culture that so profoundly affects personal and business relationships. How well you apply the lessons contained herein will determine your success in Mexico.

So do your homework, then get out there and do as your Mexican counterparts—do business!

ACKNOWLEDGMENTS

This book was made possible by the experience that both authors gained in our respective odysseys through the always fascinating and ever challenging business world of Mexico. Each of us acknowledges the many individuals who contributed to our education or assisted in the production of the book.

Roger wishes especially to thank international legal light Ed Einstein of San Antonio; Ed Ranger and Chito Padillo of Mexico City; Felipe Mondragon, former director of the Texas Department of Commerce, Mexico City office; and Dr. John McCray, NAFTA Statistician, University of Texas at San Antonio, for all the excellent information they provided.

Glenn offers thanks to Dr. Patricia Lemay Burr, Director of International Business at The University of the Incarnate Word and a practicing business owner in Mexico, for her input and encouragement; to John Skogland, a premier attorney who dedicated himself to learning about Mexico's business and legal culture, for his wisdom and support; and to Kevin Larue for designing a striking cover for this book.

A very special acknowledgment goes to Alejandro Garza Laguera of Monterrey—an international business leader and true pioneer of free trade whose knowledge, courtesy, and integrity are the bedrock upon which lasting relationships are built and whose friendship will always be cherished.

For opening the door to Cerveceria Cuauhtémoc and the marvelous adventures that followed, this book is also a tribute to the memory of Ward Wilcox, a mentor and advertising industry legend, and to George "Hal" Harker, whose integrity and loyalty were without equal and who taught us all that while *bueno* is good, there is always something better.

Both authors thank Jim Whitehead, logistician extraordinaire, who can get it from here to there on time and on budget; George Kauss, former U.S. Undersecretary of Commerce for Tourism, for his encouragement; and Joel G. Reed for his computer skills and support for some of the most tedious demands of this book.

Obviously we could not have done the job without the support and patience of our wives, Vida Reed and Judy Gray, who lost us for many a night and weekend. Last but not least, infinite thanks to Roger's mother, Mary Z. Gray, a great writer in her own right, for editing our original manuscript. Neither of us will ever again place a period outside a quotation mark.

And, finally, to Theresa May, Assistant Director and Executive Editor of University of Texas Press, whose keen wit and slightly aggressive patience spurred us to finish this book, our enduring thanks.

INTRODUCTION

Merchants have no country.
The mere spot they stand on does not
constitute so strong an attachment as
that from which they draw their gains.

THOMAS JEFFERSON, 1814

Have you always felt left out, as if all the great business opportunities have passed you by—the California gold rush, the Oklahoma land rush, IBM stock in the 1930s, Texas real estate in the early 1980s . . . ? Those were just warm-ups to Mexico in the 1990s.

But wait—hasn't the recent political and economic turmoil stopped business cold in its tracks? Temporarily slowed it, yes. Stopped it? Absolutely not!

For better or worse, Mexico has survived the vagaries of capricious politicians for many years. The Mexicans are an incredibly resilient people: despite suffering repeated political and economic reversals of colossal proportions, they pick themselves up, dust themselves off, and plow on, ever more determined to succeed.

That is precisely what is going on today.

Remember this—an entire country of 80 million souls has committed itself to a free economy by throwing off decades of protectionist barriers. Mexico has opened its doors to free trade and development and is actively seeking foreign participation in its economy. Never has the opportunity been better to jump in.

When was the best time to go into real estate in Texas, during the boom of the early 1980s or the bust at the end of that decade? Although many people made money on the way up, the real winners are those who entered the market after the crash, buying in at the bottom.

While Mexico's economy has clearly gone through a crash of its own, the basic needs remain constant: business and technological know-how, export marketing and distribution channels, strategic partners, capital investment.

Round out the portrait by picturing this nearly virgin market sharing two thousand miles of border with the richest and largest market in the world, and you can begin to understand the magnitude of opportunity awaiting you in Mexico.

All of this brings us to the sole guiding principle of this volume: if you know what you're doing, you can make a whole lot of money doing business with Mexico. And right now is the time to get in.

We'll go into more details later, but suffice it to say that Mexico is undergoing a revolution every bit as radical as that of 1910, but without the bloodshed and with winners on all sides. It's undergoing a transformation as complete as that of Eastern Europe, but with three major differences:

1. There is still a lot of money in Mexico.

2. The Mexican people have a long, solid tradition of hard work and entrepreneurial zeal.

3. Mexico shares a two-thousand-mile border with the U.S.—easy access to the world's largest market.

Now, to the purpose of this book. Mexico's a wonderful place for business, but it *is* a foreign country. They do things differently there. Not terribly differently, but enough that it matters. You can go right in and start doing business today without this book, but how much business and at what cost?

In our consulting businesses, the majority of our clients

are companies that have started working with Mexico on their own; after six months or a year of stubbing their toes, they contact us seeking guidance in the marketplace. It's not difficult once you understand some of the peculiarities of the culture and business practices. But these differences aren't particularly easy to learn without some outside help.

Our goal is not to give you some esoteric, scholarly treatise on the benefits of trade with Mexico. The benefit is money—Mexico is good business. We want to give you the basic working skills to allow you to thrive in the world of Mexican business and some practical reference information for your day-to-day use.

This is not a get-rich-quick scheme. We won't teach you how to buy real estate for no money down. Before you leap into the "romance" of business with Mexico, be prepared to make a long-term commitment. Results come gradually, and, if you've done your homework, over time they can snowball.

Mexico has gone from being one of the most hostile business climates in the world for foreigners to one of the most open and most welcoming. Vast fortunes will be created over the next few years as a result of the unique market forces unleashed by these changes.

Pent-up demand, low-cost labor, and abundant private capital are but a few of the factors driving the future of the Mexican economy and your business opportunities with it. You're already ahead of your competition—you're reading this book. Most of the U.S. is just barely waking up to the existence of Mexico as a world player. Few are seriously entering the market yet.

In your hands is the distillation of our decades of practical experience with this wonderful country and its sometimes trying business practices. Combined with your hard work, it could save you a year or more of wasted effort and untold sums of wasted money.

If you only read one chapter, read about business etiquette. This is the area we find most American business people are the weakest in. Not that we don't practice good manners in business in the U.S.—it's just that what's customary and acceptable here differs in many cases from what's practiced in Mexico. As vast and geographically insulated as the U.S. is, many of us have had little exposure to other cultures and languages and consequently are poorly prepared to adapt to a different cultural and business environment.

The better you blend in, the faster your business will progress. Sore thumbs stick out, and they're rarely appreciated. In that regard Mexico is no different than anywhere else. Your goal is to be an "insider"—one of those rare foreigners who stands out from the competition by not standing out from the locals—someone who understands and performs the sometimes intricate social ballet that is the backbone of all business and culture in this country of deep and ancient traditions.

Our goal is to help you become that perceptive foreigner who can more quickly be accepted and assimilated into the social and business milieu of Mexico.

Mexico offers probably the greatest business opportunity that any of us will see in our lifetimes. The time to step up and take advantage of this opportunity is right now. Think back to the 1950s and 1960s when "Made in Japan" was the mark of inferior products and the source of derisive jokes. Is anyone still laughing?

Throughout the decade of the 1960s, Japan and Mexico were the two fastest growing economies in the world. In the 1970s Mexico took a wrong turn politically, but it is now firmly back on the right track and gaining fast. Imagine if you had had the opportunity and the foresight to establish a market presence and to invest in Japan in those early years. Where would you be today?

Unlike Japan, Mexico is inviting you in, eagerly seeking foreign participation in its economy. With Mexico's growth potential and natural resources, it would be hard to imagine a more favorable scenario.

HOW TO DO BUSINESS
IN MEXICO

CHAPTER 1

MEXICO—
THE MARKET

A bad neighbor is a misfortune,
as much as a good one is a great blessing.

HESIOD (CA. 700 B.C.)

From a marketer's viewpoint, Mexico is a classic opportunity. The country is emerging from protectionism into a free market economy. The manufacturing sector has had limited access to current technology, facing a scarcity of certain classes of raw materials and the lack of published research identifying consumer wants versus basic needs.

Government policy created monopolies and insulated domestic producers from foreign competition, leading to inefficient production methods and a lackadaisical approach to quality control. The consumer was caught in the middle, having to choose between poor-quality, domestically produced merchandise and world-class imported goods, at prices inflated to two or three times their actual market value.

From stereos to washing machines, soap, television sets, clothing, packaged food . . . you name it, the Mexican consumer perceived the imported products to be of superior quality. Availability and price were the limiting factors.

Add to this the pent-up demand for U.S. products among Mexican youth, who avidly follow the latest trends in music and fashion via satellite television and magazines, and the market begins to take on real dimension.

Nearly all of these former import restrictions have now been dropped, and the North American Free Trade Agreement (NAFTA) addresses the remaining issues. Now is the time for you to get established in the marketplace, while this ingrained preference for foreign-made products still exists.

Mexican industry is undergoing a radical transformation of its own as it gears up to compete with the best in the world in a truly open market economy. The quality of products is improving drastically, and pricing is coming into line.

Never will you see a market opportunity better described by that old cliché "If you snooze you lose."

How Big Is It?

A primary question for anyone considering the value of doing business in Mexico versus the cost in time, effort, and dollars must be "What is the size of the market?" The answer is that it is big, not only in geography and population, but most importantly, in Gross Domestic Product (GDP) and buying power.

Mexico covers a land area of 761,065 square miles; its current population is estimated at well over 87,000,000 and growing at the rate of 2.0 percent per year. Households are increasing at the rate of one million per annum, indicating a continuing surge of youthful families establishing a homestead.

Mexico's economy, fueled by this population growth, increased from $208 billion in 1989 to $317 billion in 1992, with President Zedillo's open-market policies holding ever-growing promise for the future.

Mexican society is split into two clearly defined economic groups, rich and poor, with an emerging middle class beginning to flex its muscle. Clearly, the majority of the population is poor, but don't take that to mean that it's a poor country or an insignificant market.

First, there are some 26,000,000 consumers in Mexico with the discretionary income to readily afford U.S. products. Most are concentrated in the major cities. Mexico City's population alone includes 6,000,000 consumers in this category. These are sophisticated shoppers with an eye for quality and they are extremely brand conscious. And Mexico's rich are *really* rich.

Second, the U.S. and Mexico are already well established as primary trading partners. In 1993 Mexico surpassed Japan to become our second largest trading partner, after Canada. The U.S. is the leading exporter to Mexico, supplying 70 percent of its foreign purchases while at the same time absorbing over 67 percent of its exports.

As in the U.S., Mexico's primary markets are established centers for industry, wholesale distribution, and mass retail outlets. Mexico City is the world's most populated city and the epicenter of retail marketing in Mexico. Monterrey to the north and Guadalajara to the northwest of Mexico City are both manufacturing and retail centers as well. Characteristics of these markets are detailed in a subsequent chapter.

Mexico's terrain is as diverse as its economic makeup, ranging from desert in the north to tropical rain forests in the south and everything in between, including a mountain chain with five volcanic peaks from 9,101 feet up to 18,855 feet high.

Mexico's many charms are appropriately framed by the Gulf of Mexico on the east and the Pacific Ocean on the west. Resorts abound on both coasts, and millions of foreign tourists visit them as well as the Mexican interior on an annual basis.

THE OPPORTUNITY

The opportunity for investment and trade has never been brighter, and the benefits for both countries hold great potential—how great will depend upon the ability to read the market, create the relationships to enter the market, and understand the methods required to capture your share of the market.

Since the Salinas administration began setting the tone, the government's approach to business has become very positive and result oriented. Typical of this new attitude is a clause in the foreign investment regulations stipulating that if you have applied for permission to open or invest in certain businesses requiring Foreign Investment Commission approval, and do not receive an official response within forty-five days, the request is automatically considered granted. Bureaucratic stonewalling is no longer tolerated.

Import licensing is also being phased out. Previously required on nearly 12,000 items, licenses are now required for fewer than 200.

Also finding their way to the scrap heap are the "official import prices" imposed as a nontariff barrier at customs. These involved the arbitrary determination of the value of imports based on a schedule published by the central government. Artificially high values were assessed, thereby raising the duties by as much as 100 percent in some cases.

Now 73 percent of Mexico's economy is open to 100-percent foreign ownership, without prior governmental approval. Approval is required only in certain industries or where the investment exceeds $100 million.

In sensitive businesses where Mexican majority ownership is still required, investment trusts can be established for as long as twenty years.

The United States is by far the largest source of foreign investment in Mexico. Our accumulated investment there totaled nearly $17 billion by 1990, almost ten times that of Great Britain, which came in second, and way ahead of Japan's $1.3 billion.

While these opportunities are available for all foreign investors, the United States business community is certainly positioned by geography and historical precedent to benefit from our long established relationships with our southern neighbor.

CHAPTER 2

SEISMIC CHANGES

A lo hecho, pecho.

[Let's get going.]

Historically Mexico has been home ground to one of the most closed economies in the free world. As recently as 1987, Mexico was drowning under a foreign debt of $107 billion, *76 percent of its GNP,* and an economy crippled by interventionist policies that hindered imports and severely limited foreign investment. By 1992 foreign debt was down to 30 percent of GNP.

Longtime Mexico observers relying on historical precedent held that President Carlos Salinas de Gortari would follow the lead of his predecessors in maintaining the status quo and continue the traditional attitude toward foreign trade. They were wrong.

The 43-year-old Harvard-educated president had other plans. During his first months in office he startled the establishment by slashing import tariffs and selling off prized state-owned companies. He further shocked them by opening many heretofore closed industries to foreign investment and allowing the ownership of certain businesses by foreign interests.

Were these radical changes the actions of an ambitious politician determined to establish a prominent position in

Mexican history? Certainly that was one impression that his unheard of actions created. To global marketers, however, there emerged the carefully thought out plan of a man dedicated to stabilizing the Mexican economy and halting the free fall that began in 1982. That was the year inflation began to accelerate at the rate of 30 percent per annum and the once stable peso devalued on an almost daily basis.

The process of reopening the country's economy was begun under the administration of Miguel de la Madrid. Guided in part by his budget and planning minister, Carlos Salinas de Gortari, de la Madrid made a commitment to modernize the economy. Mexico applied for membership in the General Agreement on Trade and Tariffs (GATT, the international trade negotiating body) in 1985 and became a member the following year.

President Salinas appeared to be a man with a mission, dedicated to restoring the Mexican economy while acquiring dollars, marks, yen, and other currency through commercial trade to stabilize his own country's currency.

When Salinas took office in 1988, inflation hovered around 160 percent. In just two years it declined to 20 percent and the peso had been restabilized. Year-end 1993 showed inflation dropping below 10 percent, a reduction of over 150 percent in just five years. To understand the enormity of these dramatic changes and the strength of President Salinas' commitment to a free market economy, we must take at least a brief look at Mexico's past.

Spain invaded Mexico in 1519 and ruled the country as a colony for the next 300 years. Ancient civilizations that had flourished for centuries such as the Aztec, Mixtec, and Zapotec were overwhelmed. Their priests and chieftains were killed, imprisoned, or banished, and the Spanish language, religion, and culture were force-fed to a reluctant people. But, no matter how severe the oppressors, a proud people will not endure domination forever, and the fight for independence began in 1810. Eleven years later, in 1821, Spain's stranglehold was broken. On October 4, 1824,

Mexico assumed its present name and declared itself a republic.

As the battle scars of the new republic healed, growing pains set in, and in 1836 most of the land that is now Texas was lost at the battle of San Jacinto near present-day Houston. In 1848 this loss was further compounded when, after being defeated by invading U.S. troops, Antonio López de Santa Anna sold a vast area that included lands in what are now the states of California, Arizona, Colorado, New Mexico, Texas, and Utah to the U.S. This constituted one-half of the territory of Mexico, to say nothing of being some of its richest land.

In the Mexican psyche, this coerced sale remains a source of resentment against their strong-armed northern neighbor. The final battle of the war which brought this all about is still the stuff of legends and heroes for both nations today. "The Halls of Montezuma" of the U.S. Marine Corps hymn was in fact the National Palace of Mexico. That last battle ended when the remaining army cadets defending the palace wrapped themselves in the Mexican flag and threw themselves over the balcony, rather than accept defeat at the hands of a foreign invader. You will see in almost every town in Mexico a street or a monument to the "Niños Héroes," the boy heroes of this legend.

How's that for a foundation on which to build good neighborly relations?

Subsequently, Mexico was invaded by the French, who installed as emperor Maximilian of Hapsburg. He was ousted and executed in 1867 and was soon replaced by Benito Juárez.

A long period of development by foreign interests flourished under the dictator Porfirio Díaz. This second incursion into Mexican homelands by foreigners helped foment the bloody revolution that began in 1910. The full thrust of this political and social upheaval was realized in 1938 when the country's basic industries were expropriated by Mexico's new government.

Like that of many other Latin American countries, Mexico's economy was structured around import substitution policies, limitations on foreign investment, and an officially controlled currency exchange rate. The expressed goal was to encourage the growth of domestic industry and to ward off the perceived threat of foreign economic domination. The actual result, though, was quite the opposite.

Mexico's dedication to nationalization of private interests has manifested itself in recent years as well, with privately held land being expropriated by the government and redistributed. The government takeover of all banks in 1983 generated a flight of Mexico's privately held capital that stunned the marketplace.

Mexico's constitution gives the government authority to seize control of businesses in "strategic" sectors. This loose terminology has led over the years to government ownership of a wide range of businesses, which, as you can imagine, were not run at the peak of efficiency by government bureaucrats. By the end of 1982, the government owned or controlled 1,155 "parastatal" businesses, ranging from the telephone system to bicycle factories, restaurants, and banks.

Against this background, the actions of President de la Madrid and his successor, Carlos Salinas, took on heroic dimensions in their scope and vision and signaled a decisive new direction for this historic country. By the end of June 1991, the number of state-owned businesses was down to 269 and shrinking fast.

Former sacred cows such as Telmex (the phone company), the copper mine at Cananea, and the two national airlines have been sold to consortiums with strong participation by foreign companies. As of June 1991, the banks were beginning to be sold off to private investment groups. The only two entities that the government insists will remain under its control are Pemex (the national petroleum company) and the Federal Electrical Commission.

Even with all of this good news, the best is yet to come

for the North American business community. NAFTA links the United States, Canada, and Mexico in an economic alliance that holds enormous implications for business growth throughout the continent. Creating new opportunities for trade, jobs, and an improved competitive stance against the established trading partnerships in Europe and Asia is the principal thrust of this agreement.

In this effort, President Salinas took the initiative, seeking to expand on the foundation of the U.S.-Canada Free Trade Agreement. He overcame decades of xenophobia to thrust Mexico into the forefront of world trade in a firm alliance with its continental neighbors.

SALINASTROIKA

During the heady days of the *apertura* or opening of Mexico's markets under President Salinas, Mexicans affectionately referred to the process as "Salinastroika," a New World equivalent of the *perestroika* in the former Soviet Union. Although Salinas undeniably changed Mexico's role in the world, his place in the history books faces a serious challenge.

It became painfully apparent upon his departure that Salinas had artificially propped up the Mexican economy during the last year or two of his administration. Within days of assuming power, President Zedillo was forced to devalue the peso, triggering a crisis in confidence in the Mexican government. This lack of confidence, more than the economic conditions, set off an economic collapse reminiscent of 1982.

As accusations and recriminations were hurled at Salinas for his gross mismanagement of the economy, his brother Raúl was arrested for involvement in the political assassination of his former brother-in-law. Reports have since tied Raúl intimately to the drug cartels which grew immensely powerful during his brother's rule.

Common wisdom in Mexico assumes that the former president was a witting participant in the alleged corruption for which his brother stands accused. Few believe that Raúl would or could carry out his nefarious activities without the blessings of his omnipotent brother. Whether historians focus more on the enormous advances Salinas brought to Mexico or his considerable fall from grace remains to be seen.

CHAPTER 3

WHEN IN ROME

When in Rome, do as the Romans do.
(universally good advice, and
especially applicable to Mexico)

In order to thrive in business in Mexico, you have to become culturally fluent and blend in socially. We may be close geographically, but our cultural differences can make us seem worlds apart.

"Poor Mexico, so far from God, yet so close to the United States." Thus has Mexico long viewed its gigantic, overweight, clumsy, sometimes violent, always greedy next-door neighbor. The U.S. has been vilified in the institutional sense by government, unions, academics, et al. for being a fickle friend, never letting loose with the largesse offered to more distant allies—an unwelcome neighbor to snub and avoid as much as possible in official dealings.

A somewhat lopsided view to be sure, but not without foundation. The U.S. did after all invade Mexico in the last century and grab nearly half of its territory. And again in this century, we sent an expeditionary force, headed by General "Black Jack" Pershing, to hunt down Pancho Villa inside of Mexico and, in a related action, occupied the port of Veracruz.

Mexicans live by tradition and history, a fact one can never overlook in business. None have forgotten and many have never forgiven the U.S. for these transgressions of their sovereignty.

The changes in attitude and policy of the Salinas administration abruptly thawed relations between our governments in the political equivalent of the greenhouse effect. On the personal level, relations have always been warm between individual Mexicans and Americans. We have generally been very well received one on one.

The anti-*yanqui* posturing of past administrations was not necessarily a reflection of popular sentiment, but more of political ideology and demagoguery. Nevertheless, while political harangues of the past may not have represented the individuals' views, the Mexicans are deeply patriotic and well versed in their country's history.

Always bear in mind that the Mexican memory is long, and there is a free exchange among colleagues of information regarding who is reliable and who is not in the business world, especially outsiders.

Although no description of the culture and attitudes of any country can possibly hold true 100 percent of the time for everyone in that country, certain aspects can be generalized. While the suggestions we offer in this section may tend culturally toward a more conservative approach to business, if you start from this basis you will never find yourself an outcast by virtue of having offended or unduly shocked your hosts and colleagues.

PATIENCE IS ITS OWN REWARD

Good advice when embarking upon any new venture in a foreign land is *be patient.* Mexico is no exception. While you'll have every opportunity to exercise your aggressive competitiveness, adopt the tortoise's mentality, and not the hare's. International trade is *not* for short-term players. Relations and trust have to be established over time. You are unlikely to see quick results in Mexico, particularly early on in a relationship.

Attributing this indisposition by Mexicans toward leap-ing into a business relationship as an indication of lack of ag-gression or business savvy could be a serious mistake. This misconception has cost many a gringo his shirt. Mexicans have a saying *Del tonto vive el vivo*—the smart man makes a living off the fool.

There are few negotiators anywhere who can out-deal Mexican business people. Their deliberate, cautious ap-proach in opening up to strangers is based on a variety of fac-tors. One is simply that they want to know with whom they're dealing. What are your real capabilities and capaci-ties? Can you be trusted? Who are you socially? A lot of it is just a trial period to see if you'll be around for the long term or if, like many of your compatriots before you, you're just here to sell them a bill of goods and disappear, never to be seen again.

Here is where the benefits of patience will pay healthy dividends. Friendships, once made, are taken seriously and backed with a degree of commitment not always seen on our side of the border.

A CPA friend in San Antonio got a call from a longtime client, inviting him to Mexico City to discuss the possibility of providing consulting and accounting services on a $100 million project. He took off immediately for Mexico City.

Over the course of a three-hour lunch the client never once mentioned the project, talking instead about personal matters and carrying on social conversation. The client then asked our CPA friend to drive around Mexico City with him to visit some properties that he owned, once again never mentioning the big deal. Finally, six hours later, after dinner, the intrepid CPA brought up the subject he'd been invited down to discuss. The client said, "Of course, I'm going to let you handle this deal. You are my friend and I trust you."

That was it. The remaining business arrangements were covered in fifteen minutes, and then back to the social visit.

On the basis of friendship and trust, this accountant picked up a $100 million account. Putting that business up for bid was never even considered. Because he had proved himself over time as a friend and valued business associate, it was perfectly natural for the client to award him this huge project.

Once you've established a personal relationship, people will naturally refer you to others within their circle of family and peers. The "old boy network" is at the core of Mexican business. Once you've entered the inner circles, doors open and busy executives suddenly find time for you. Appointments will be easy to make, and a receptive ear awaits your proposal.

Once it's made, your reputation sticks with you, so proceed with care. Before you make commitments be sure you can fulfill them. *Lo prometido es deuda*—a promise is a debt. This is good business anywhere, but in Mexico failure to produce on a promise can brand you permanently. Word of a good deal travels fast, of a bad deal even faster.

Social and business circles are fairly small, and industry leaders are all well known and circulate socially with each other. Wealthy families often are widely diversified, with many business interests. Family connections are strong. A solid performance in one area can open the doors to a vast array of opportunities elsewhere.

Adjust Your Attitude

Before you set foot in Mexico, adjust your attitude. The standard American approach to business—shake hands, roll up your sleeves, lay out the numbers, cut a deal—is rarely the path to success in this cautious environment.

Although there is a new generation of aggressive young business people in Mexico, many of whom have been educated in the U.S. or Europe, the conservative approach is always correct until they show you otherwise. Traditional first-time meetings are focused more on establishing personal rapport than on crunching numbers.

The first-time meeting with your Mexican contact will probably be a social occasion. Try to get through it without immediately pressing for business. Don't worry—business will be discussed, but let your counterpart take the lead.

You may also find yourself dealing with one of the new generation who hasn't the time to waste on social preliminaries and tells you so or lets you know in one fashion or another. Once the ground rules have been set, step right up and play.

Americans tend to always keep an eye on the clock. We schedule appointments in rapid-fire succession and cut meetings and conversations short to accommodate our next appointment. This rarely is the custom in Mexico.

The Mexican sense of time is more flexible than ours. Arriving at 10:30 for a 10:00 appointment is not even cause for comment. Not that you should arrive late for your appointments—just don't schedule yourself so tightly that delayed starts to earlier meetings or extended conversations will jeopardize later activities. And *don't* keep looking at your watch! That is considered the height of rudeness.

SCHEDULING YOUR DAYS

The typical Mexican workday schedule is as follows:

8:00 or 9:00–10:00 A.M.	Breakfast
10:00 A.M.–2:00 P.M.	Office hours
2:00–4:00 or 5:00 P.M.	Lunch
4:30–6:00 or 7:00 P.M. +	Office hours
7:00–9:00 P.M.	Available for cocktail appt.
9:00–Midnight +	Dinner hours

When you're trying to reach executives by phone, it may seem that they work an awfully light schedule, coming in at

10:00 A.M. and taking off for two or three hours for lunch; because you've gone home by the time they get back from lunch, you may imagine that their day is over too. While that may be the impression from a distance, the above schedule is a more accurate description of a typical executive's workday.

Dinner is more likely to be reserved for friends and close associates and often is at home. The rest of the day, from breakfast through lunch and into the evening, is all valid time for business, a great deal of which is conducted out of the office. Hence your difficulty in reaching executives by phone.

When scheduling appointments, allow yourself plenty of leeway. You've traveled a long way and spent a good bit of money to get there, so give yourself adequate time to make the most out of each appointment. Allow at least two hours as a minimum for each meeting. And don't forget to factor in traffic delays, especially in Mexico City.

In Mexico City, for instance, at midday it can take an hour or more to drive from the Polanco area, where the Nikko, Presidente, and Camino Real hotels are, to the Pedregal district, on the south side of town. In the four rush hours (coming and going to lunch creates another pair of rush hours), the same journey can take twice that or more.

While not quite as congested, Monterrey and Guadalajara have such traffic periods as well. Whether driving yourself or traveling by taxi, the traffic must be factored into your travel time.

It is also wise to make allowances in your schedule for appointments that may start half an hour or forty-five minutes late. This used to be the norm, but fortunately it is a rapidly disappearing practice. In the past, especially in government offices, an individual's importance was gauged by how long you had to wait.

For a real big shot this could literally be measured in hours. It was not at all unusual to arrive on time for an appointment, take a seat in the outer office, and sit for hours as the secretary went in and out with coffee, the newspaper, etc. You might get an occasional glimpse of the person you came to see, reading the newspaper or chatting with buddies who came and went while you sat and waited. Thank heavens this attitude is nearly extinct.

CHAPTER 4

MAKING CONTACT

It isn't what you know,
it's *who* you know.

So, now that you've prepared yourself in a general sense, how do you make the first contacts for business? And most importantly, with whom?

Before we go into how, it's vital to understand the "with whom." Mexico in a very real sense has a caste system. Unlike the system in India, you can move up or down the social ladder by success or failure in business, but the divisions are clearly understood by all the players. You deal with your equals. Generally, an important industrialist will not have direct dealings with anyone's sales manager. If you want access to top management, plan on making the contacts yourself.

In most cases, major business decisions are made only at the top. Buyers and mid-level managers are rarely vested with the authority to commit to projects or contract with new suppliers. They are not decision makers.

Unfortunately, the fragility of their macho self-image won't allow them to tell you that they don't have the authority to make a deal or to give you a clean "no." If you don't understand the system going in, you can be led on and on and on, while never reaching a conclusion.

If you deal with a purchasing agent or mid-level manager or official, you aren't likely to reach the chief executive, who actually makes the decisions. You will be judged by the level at which you approach the company.

An important executive in Mexico would never start at the bottom and work up. You must do the same if you expect to be taken seriously. Simply put, initiate and conduct your business dealings at the highest possible level. *If you open negotiations with underlings, that is probably as high a level as you will ever effectively reach.*

Networking is everything in Mexico. Your ultimate success will depend on who you know. As mentioned earlier, the social and business circles are relatively small in any given city, and particularly tight within a given industry. If you are introduced at the right level to the right people, you are considered an equal—and doors will open.

A personal introduction through a mutual friend or acquaintance is undoubtedly the quickest route in. Of course, the closer the friend, the warmer the reception. Cold calling is probably the least effective means of accessing top executives and officials.

Absent an established network of friends or associates, there are several avenues of entree. One, of course, is to hire a consultant who can make the introductions for you. This is the method we use, and it provides quick access and better results for our clients.

If you have a Mexican embassy or consulate near you, present your business credentials and objectives to the ambassador, consul general, or trade attaché first and find out what help they can give you. A letter of introduction from one of these officials can open many doors.

Clubs and associations provide great entree to top business people as well. One of the best of these groups is the Rotary Club. Rotarians are a select group in Mexico, and as a visiting member you are immediately welcomed as a peer.

Another great "in" is participation in any officially sanctioned activity (Sister Cities delegations, chamber of commerce trips, governmental groups, etc.). Much stock is placed in official standing and titles in Mexico.

NETWORKING THE CHAMBERS

The Mexican chambers of commerce and industry are especially powerful organizations and offer fertile hunting grounds for contacts.

Mexican law has long mandated that every business *must* belong to one of the officially sanctioned chambers of commerce or industry. In order to renew your business license in Mexico each year, you have to show your chamber dues receipt.

Rumors persist of eliminating the obligatory nature of chamber membership, but so far the status quo remains. There is much speculation as to the effect of this rule change, but it is safe to assume that chamber memberships would plummet throughout the country. It will be interesting to see if, in an open, voluntary, and competitive market, the official chambers can compete with the more active voluntary groups, such as Am-Cham (the American Chamber of Commerce) and CONACEX (the National Foreign Trade Council).

How this change would affect these organizations' political clout is anyone's guess. The following information and suggestions are based on the status quo.

While there are dozens of specialized chambers, the two main ones are CANACINTRA, the chamber of industry, and CANACO, the chamber of commerce. CANACINTRA represents eleven major industrial manufacturing sectors and has over 86,000 members. CANACO represents mostly retail merchants and the tourism industry, and the Mexico City chapter alone has over 50,000 members.

Each classification of industry or business has its own council within these massive organizations, allowing you to target your activities with remarkable accuracy. There are also numerous single-industry chambers, such as the National Chamber for the Shoe Industry or the National Chamber for the Oils, Greases, and Soap Industry.

In addition to government-sanctioned chambers, there are a number of voluntary membership chambers and organizations that are well worth your attention. The strongest two in this category are the American Chamber of Commerce and CONACEX. The members of both these organizations are highly focused on international trade.

Am-Cham began in Mexico City as a chamber for the American companies doing business in Mexico. Now more than two-thirds of its 3,000+ members are Mexican companies involved or interested in foreign trade. They put out some excellent publications about business in Mexico and sponsor many trade-related activities. Business is conducted in English, so you'll feel right at home.

Because of their dedication to one business discipline, the Mexican chambers are rich with pertinent information regarding industry trends, strengths, and needs that can provide you with a wealth of facts regarding industry opportunities as well as a forum for contacts. Once you have determined which chamber pertains to the type of business you are pursuing, you can rest assured that the leaders in that sector will constitute the executives of that chamber. For a directory of Mexico's chambers of commerce and industry, see Appendix I.

Not to be overlooked in your dealings with the chambers is the incredible political muscle of these groups. The national presidents of CANACO and CANACINTRA have direct access to the president, the cabinet, and all levels of officialdom. If you have a project requiring government involvement, or are just seeking access to high officials, sell your idea to top chamber executives first—they can provide the entree into the halls of government.

THE VALUE OF GOVERNMENTAL CONTACTS

Proper contacts in various departments of government can be vital to your success; therefore it is important that you not fall victim to flawed first impressions concerning the role of government in business. You will find that most Mexican business people, much like their U.S. counterparts, tend to be scornful of the effectiveness of political officials in general and allege that they want as little to do with government as possible. Yet, in Mexico, when a cabinet official, governor, or mayor proclaims a new program, those same business people are off like a bolt of lightning, racing to see who can be first on the scene to lend a hand and participate in the program.

There is a reason for this; no political office in the United States can compare in terms of raw power to that wielded by chief executive officials in Mexico. From the president of the local chamber of commerce, to the mayor, to the governor, to the president of Mexico, top elected officials preside as if over a fiefdom. With a nod of the head, the impossible is resolved. With a wave of a hand, armies of workers are put in motion.

The president, on a swing through the countryside, stops in a rural village and hears from local leaders about their lack of services and sense of isolation. Before the year is out, they have a new paved road, a clinic, and a water treatment plant—things for which they had petitioned through normal channels for years. No appropriation request, no budget hearings, no red tape—an order from the president is all it takes.

A group of business leaders in Veracruz wanted us to hold a trade exhibition in their new convention center. They had lined up support from local and state government officials in favor of the idea. But nobody would commit or make any move; until the governor himself gave it the nod, the project was in limbo.

Then, just two weeks before a major show in San Antonio, we received a call from Veracruz saying that a meeting had been set with the governor for the day after tomorrow! Breaking away from frenzied, last-minute show preparations, Roger made the vital trek. He was ushered into the governor's majestic office in Xalapa, and there assembled were the business leaders who had invited us, three state cabinet officers, two state legislators, and assorted functionaries—all on the edge of their seats awaiting the governor's verdict on the exhibition.

After a brief presentation, the governor smiled, nodded, and said it looked like a great project for the state. Looking directly at the state secretary of commerce, he said, "Make it happen." With that, all the players fell in line—TV commercials produced and aired on the state-owned TV station, posters printed at state expense, concessions galore, and access to any and everyone we needed to make it happen.

So, regardless of what you hear, official contacts are of tremendous help to any business effort. Another benefit is that your credibility within the business community goes up proportionally to the depth and breadth of your access to government officials.

We were invited by the Chamber of Industry of Guadalajara to take a booth in its industrial expo one year, with the purpose of promoting one of our shows. We had met with the top officials of the chamber and had begun a cordial relationship, but had not yet really established our bona fides with them. The state governor inaugurated their expo and then made a round of the booths, waving to the exhibitors as he passed. When he reached our booth, he stopped, his face lit up, and he threw his arms around each of us in a big *abrazo* (a formal hug—the warmest form of personal greeting) and stayed to talk for five minutes.

With all of the chamber officials and assorted VIPs gathered around, this was the most powerful credential we could have presented. From that moment forward, the relationship with the chamber officials quickly transformed into a warm personal friendship. We have continued to do business and remain friends to this day, but the act that erased any doubts about our legitimacy was that public greeting from the governor. (For a listing of key government agencies, see Chapter 13.)

OFFICIAL GIFT GIVING

Gifts are traditionally exchanged during formal ceremonies, especially during official visits by governmental authorities. Typical gifts are regional handcrafts, books, or pieces of art.

If you are in the position of offering a gift in a public ceremony, you need to be aware of a delicate point of protocol, especially if the gift is being given to a government official. The gift should always be given mounted on a presentation board and wrapped in clear, shrink-wrap plastic so that everyone can see what it is when it's given.

You can have this done at most department stores. The reason for this type of packaging is that clear plastic leaves no question as to what sort of gift is being given or received. Presenting a gift in an opaque wrapper may be perceived as an attempt to hide the nature of the object; therefore the situation is always handled as described.

This is a standard and acceptable method to follow with any business gift exchange—and if a government official at any level is the recipient it is the only accepted protocol.

CHAPTER 5

SOCIAL GRACES

> Without society,
> and a society to our taste,
> men are never contented.
>
> THOMAS JEFFERSON

As a visiting foreigner you may be excused for lapses in social form, but if you wish to be accepted as a true business and social equal, take the time and effort to assume the local habits of grace and charm.

Men should always, always, always show the *utmost* respect when dealing with women. This is never a laughing matter. The most rigid rules of etiquette apply to all contact with women, especially the wives of business associates.

When a woman enters or leaves the room, all men stand immediately (and we do mean stand, not a halfhearted halfrise). The same holds true when a woman comes or goes at the dining table. While this may seem antiquated, or to some even chauvinistic, in the cultural context it is merely adherence to accepted customs and good manners. Old World etiquette is still de rigueur in Mexico.

Entertaining and social invitations are subject to a strict set of rules as well. First rule: whoever extends the invitation pays. There is no wrangling for the check at a restaurant. If you were invited out, don't risk offending your host by offering to pay. Likewise, if you made the invitation, plan on paying the entire bill. As a social concept, Dutch treat has not yet raised its ugly head in Mexico and we hope it never will.

Rule number two: a woman *never* pays. This is not open to interpretation. If you are a woman executive wishing to entertain clients, there are only a few options available to you. The simplest is to be accompanied by a male who picks up the check. This could be an employee, a friend, or a spouse.

You can also create a circumstance that does not imply a personal invitation to a restaurant. For instance, your *company* could hold a luncheon or a cocktail party for a group of executives, with the entire program catered in the special event salon of a restaurant or hotel. Make arrangements to prepay or settle the bill after all have left, but *never* in front of your guests.

By contemporary U.S. standards this appears discriminatory in the extreme, but in this socially correct and formal society these unwritten rules are the manifestations of good manners. Form rules, period. Some of these customs regarding women in business are evolving, but until and unless you know the people you're dealing with well, our advice is to stay traditional.

If you breach these standards of conduct, it is unlikely that anyone will comment or complain. But, mysteriously, you will find that phone calls are no longer being returned— the warm welcome you received seems to have chilled and your business progress to have frozen.

In the U.S. you would approach the proper party to determine what had gone awry, but not in Mexico. Direct confrontation is avoided at all costs. If you have offended someone, he or she will never tell you how and why. The door is closed—permanently—and it is time to move on to the next contact.

This is as good a place as any to mention that smoking is as commonplace in Mexico as in most parts of Europe. Non-smoking areas are almost unknown in buildings or restaurants. The only thing harder to find than a nonsmoking area would be a Mexican willing to join you there. Even if you're a rabid antismoker, bite the bullet and learn to withstand it. If you're in Mexico City a good old-fashioned smoke-filled room may be a distinct relief from the smog outside.

GREETINGS

Form is everything in personal greetings. You can learn much about relationships in Mexico just by observing how people greet each other.

The least personal greeting is the standard handshake. This is the greeting used when meeting strangers or casual acquaintances. It is also the appropriate greeting for someone of significantly higher social, business, or official standing to use when greeting a subordinate or someone of lower standing. Until you've established some ongoing relationships, offer and expect a handshake.

Between friends, peers, and relatives, an *abrazo* is expected. This greeting hug has several degrees to it. At its warmest, it consists of a firm hug, followed by three manly pats on the back with the right hand, which then comes around to grip in a firm handshake, with the left hand lingering on the shoulder or elbow. Don't worry about "getting it right." You'll have plenty of opportunity to observe the ritual before you're greeted this way. But don't shy away either when you are greeted this way. The guy isn't going to kiss you—this is a compliment and clear sign of friendship. See who initiates the *abrazo*, how warm it seems, how closely they embrace, and how long they hold it.

Every *abrazo* is a statement. If the mayor greets another political official or a businessman at a reception, everyone looks to see if the mayor embraces him in a warm display of friendship or gives a perfunctory half-hug and handshake. A big *abrazo* to a relative unknown could signify substantial acceptance, an opening of opportunities, while a less warm greeting to, say, a top chamber official could point to a conflict or falling out.

Greetings between two women or between a man and a woman are subject to similar gradations. At its simplest level, a nod or almost half-bow acknowledges an introduction, without any personal commitment. Next up the line comes a genteel handshake. Continuing up in warmth comes the *beso*, a peck on the cheek, more just a brushing of cheek to cheek. This is done while holding both hands. Again, the warmth and duration are determined by the closeness of the relationship.

The simple rule to follow on when and how to give *abrazos* and *besos* is simply to let the other party lead the way. It's just like being a good dance partner—let them lead, follow the steps, and try not to step on their toes. There's nothing as publicly embarrassing as being rebuffed in your attempt to greet the governor with a full *abrazo*. Beyond being embarrassing, it shows you up as a *presumido*, someone who imagines himself to be more than he is.

After you have observed and experienced it enough to comprehend the ritual, you will know when and where it's appropriate to make the first move and how warm the greeting ought to be.

INVITATIONS TO THE HOME

If you hit it off particularly well with someone, you may be invited home for dinner. Personal invitations to someone's home are not to be taken lightly. This is the ultimate compliment to you. Home and family are sacred in Mexico. To be invited into this intimate, private realm means you have already been accepted as *gente de confianza*, a person in whom one can have confidence and trust. Should you refuse the invitation, you may never again be asked: *El que nunca va a tu casa, en la suya no te quiere*—he who never goes to your home doesn't want you in his.

Dinner starts late and goes even later. If you're asked to arrive at nine, it will be for cocktails first, with the meal service no earlier than ten or ten-thirty. There is no such thing as a light meal in Mexico, and entertaining company requires the best and the most. Be prepared for cocktails, several food courses, wines, dessert, coffee, brandies, etc., and, of course, good conversation extending well into the night. It's not at all unusual for a pleasant dinner gathering to finally wrap up around two in the morning. *Best advice: drink slowly and don't keep looking at your watch!*

You will find that doing business in Mexico is an absolute delight socially. These are the most cultured, well-mannered, and gracious people you will ever meet. But therein lie some dangers for the hard-hitting, no-nonsense, guileless gringo.

NAMES, TITLES, AND FORMS OF ADDRESS

Titles are an extremely important aspect of life and business in Mexico. While in the U.S. we recognize and use very few titles as forms of address (Doctor, Professor, Reverend), Mexican society is quite keen on recognizing the positions and accomplishments of schooling and business. This is in fact a great aid in business if you have trouble remembering names. As long as you get the title right, you can very properly address people solely by their title. This shows respect and shows that you are more cultured than many of your compatriots.

The most common title used is *licenciado* (lee-sen-see-áh-doe). This literally means licensed and is applied to anyone with a technical degree, from attorneys to nurses. *Licenciado* is abbreviated in correspondence and on business cards as "Lic." Such titles are used either alone or together with the last name: "Good morning, licenciado" or "Good morning, Lic. Martínez."

Highly placed officials are always addressed and referred to (almost reverentially) by their position—Sr. Gobernador, Sr. Presidente, General, Sr. Secretario, etc.

Other specific titles include Ing. or *ingeniero* (een-hain-ee-aír-oh), for engineer; Dr. or *doctor*, the same in both languages; Arq. or *arquitecto*, for architect; and C.P. or *contador público*, for a CPA. These titles always appear on business cards and correspondence.

Last but far from least is the term *Don* (masculine) or *Doña* (feminine). These are not titles in the professional sense, but terms of respect for an older person of high standing. *Don* or *Doña* is always used with the person's first name, as in "Good afternoon, Don Ramón." Save this form, though, until you've met the person in an intimate social setting or have had repeated contact. While it shows respect, it also implies some degree of familiarity.

In formal presentations of a respected older person, the full name and both the title and *Don* are used, with the title preceding: "Lic. Don Ramón García Martínez."

This brings us to the next point—names. How are you supposed to know which is his or her last name? It's really pretty easy. All Mexicans have a first name, two last names, and usually a middle name. For men and single women, their father's last name comes first, followed by their mother's maiden name.

Using the example above of Lic. Don Ramón García Martínez, García is his father's last name and therefore *his* last name. Martínez was his mother's maiden name. In less formal terms you would address him as Ramón García. *Do not take these matters of address lightly.* Ramón García Martínez is *not* Ramón Martínez and will not appreciate being thus addressed.

When a woman marries, she drops her mother's maiden name and adds her new husband's last name after her family name. This new last name is now preceded by the word *de*, meaning "of," to denote her attachment to her husband.

To illustrate this transformation, when María Hernández Torres (call her María Hernández) married Ramón García, she became María Hernández de García. Simply put, she is now María García, though you would always address her as Señora García. Out of respect for her age, as she is the wife of Don Ramón, you could also call her Doña María.

Got all that memorized? Don't worry—we have included a handy reference table in Appendix II.

CHAPTER 6

COMMUNICATING

> "¿Aló, you speak Espaneesh . . . ?"
> Click, buzzzzz . . .
> "Hey there, you habla Inglish . . . ?"
> Click, buzzzzz . . .

BREAKING THE LANGUAGE BARRIER

Spanish is one of the easiest languages to learn, and a working knowledge of it will enhance your business prospects in Mexico tremendously. Unfortunately, it's the rare gringo who takes the time and effort, and fewer still who speak it well.

Any effort you put forth toward learning the language will be repaid in spades. The mere fact that you have gone to the trouble to show the concern and courtesy to learn your host's idiom will be very well received. But don't let it go to your head. Until you really are fluent, hire a translator for business.

Many of the business leaders you will come in contact with in Mexico already speak fluent English, thereby solving the immediate communications problem. But even if you know your contact speaks English, it can be very much in your best interests to have your own interpreter available. Suppose your bilingual Mexican colleague wants you to meet some friends or gives you a lead to another potential client. What if your contact's command of English doesn't really cover any technical terminology? How are you going to handle these issues without a translator?

Many in our office speak Spanish fluently, but we are all native English speakers. While we can converse freely in person or over the phone and indeed give speeches in Spanish in Mexico, we never lose sight of the difference between a native speaker and a foreigner fluent in the language.

In written communications, unless it's just a quick memo or a letter to a close friend, we always have a native Mexican polish the translation for us. This is particularly important in letters to government officials, dignitaries, or high-level business leaders. Be aware also that there is a difference between Mexican Spanish and the Spanish spoken in other Spanish-speaking countries. If you want it to sound Mexican, hire a Mexican.

Stop and think: what is your reaction to poorly written correspondence in English? You immediately classify the sender as less qualified and less intelligent based on a poor grasp of the language. If the correspondence comes from overseas, you may cut them some slack due to the translation issue. But aren't *you* impressed when you see foreign correspondence or literature done in flawless English? It shows you that you're dealing with a professional who has resources and has taken the time and effort to do a first-class job. Isn't this the image you want to project?

If you receive a letter in English, it's perfectly correct to respond in English. But if you're offering the first communication, or are responding to a letter in Spanish, write it in Spanish.

Where do you find good translators? Ask someone who is already doing business with Mexico. If that doesn't satisfy your needs, try a local university. Many have excellent language programs and capable students eager for the work. Last but not least, look in the yellow pages.

At our trade shows in Mexico, we have always had translators available for hire. Nearly everyone hires them. What's the point of spending two or three thousand dollars to exhibit in a trade show, but then "economizing" by not hiring a hundred-dollar-a-day translator?

Everyday business is the same. It's expensive getting to and from Mexico to do business. Make the most out of it by fully understanding what's being discussed and what the other side is saying. A good translator will vastly improve your chances of doing business by making your message clear.

Be aware, though, that not all translators were created equal. Translation is not an exact science. As there are many ways of expressing the same idea in English, likewise there are many ways in Spanish, and equally many ways to translate one to the other. A misinterpretation of a key word can lead to a completely erroneous translation.

We once were asked to review a food company's sales brochure (after it had been printed) that had been translated into Spanish by one of the company's local South Texas "bilingual" staff. Among the numerous errors was a listing for *pulpo de aguacate*. What they were trying to say was avocado pulp. There's a small, yet significant difference between the word *pulpa*, meaning pulp, and *pulpo*, meaning octopus. For some reason the *frozen avocado octopus* did not sell well!

In another case, a major fast-food client was preparing Spanish menus to put up behind the counters in their restaurants. They proudly showed us this new development (fortunately before the menus were installed), where the reference to a fresh roll had been translated literally as *rollo*. The word *rollo* in Spanish has zero to do with bread—in fact, in common colloquial usage, *rollo* means a big hassle.

These are good examples of why skilled translators are worth their weight in gold. Imagine the above scenarios in the context of a business meeting. You think you've gotten your point across, or come to terms on a key issue, only to find that your ideas were never communicated accurately or that your client's response was literally misinterpreted. You walk out of the meeting thinking that everything is on track and later discover that, in effect, two conversations had taken place—yours and your client's.

The worst part about this whole scenario is that because the misunderstanding is so fundamental whatever deal you were working on most likely will never come to fruition. One side is expecting results based on a nonexistent agreement, while the other side never has understood what was discussed. Or, based on the translation, both sides are content that they've understood each other, when in fact both have been on completely different wavelengths. In the end, both sides go their separate ways thinking that the other is deranged, dishonest, or at the very least a lousy business person.

This may sound far-fetched, but in truth it happens fairly frequently. We can't tell you how many official functions we've sat through with simultaneous translators, understanding both sides of the translation, wondering what strange image must be forming in the monolingual audience's minds as a result of bizarre interpretations of the basic principle of the talk.

If you're in a specialized business (and who isn't these days?), you may want to find a translator familiar with the technical terms of your particular field, whether it be medicine, banking, engineering, or whatever. If you're participating in a trade show, plan to spend a few hours ahead of show time with your translator to bring him or her up to speed on your products, policies, goals, and terminology. It may cost you a few extra bucks in salary, but it will be money well spent.

When you need a translator for business negotiations, hire your own. Don't rely on your potential client or supplier to provide a person with your best interests at heart or one who is necessarily a qualified translator. You want to understand clearly the entire conversation and, where possible, the tone and mood of the words being said.

A simple rule for getting everything across accurately

when using a translator is to speak slowly, clearly, and in short phrases. The real pros keep their presentations simple and direct, broken into easily translated phrases. If you ramble on, quoting figures and statistics without pausing, be absolutely assured that your message will be lost.

A perfect example of this was a recent speech in San Antonio welcoming a visiting delegation headed by the governor of a Mexican state. In his opening remarks the Texas politico spoke eloquently, but nonstop, about the long relationships between the region and Mexico, citing figures and statistics and relating all of this back to why it was such a particular honor to welcome this distinguished delegation to town. After about five minutes he finally paused for the translator, who by then had a thoroughly glazed look on his face. Unable to translate and memorize such a vast and eloquent text, the translator told the guests that the speaker said it was an honor to have them here—period. Five minutes of eloquent speech completely wasted on its intended audience.

Whether it's public speaking or private negotiations, talk with your translator before starting to work. Practice some speech to get a feel for the rhythm of breaks and length of phrasing that your translator is comfortable with. If you extend beyond his or her capability to translate and memorize, content will necessarily be lost.

During the course of negotiations, write all numbers out on paper. Don't trust translators on this key point. When it appears that you're both in agreement on terms, ask questions. Don't assume that you're both agreeing to the same thing. Clarify every point to assure that you both understand what's taking place. The mutual understanding we take for granted when conducting business at home can't be assumed when crossing the language frontier.

Language is both a bridge and a barrier. Picture it as a drawbridge. When you've taken the effort to insure good communications, the bridge is lowered in invitation and traffic flows with ease. Without proper communications, the bridge is lifted and traffic, faced with a moat filled with dragons, comes to a halt.

Set yourself apart from the crowd, show respect for the people you're doing business with, and make your investment in time and money pay off by taking the language difference seriously. You'll find that not everyone does—and that offers you the chance to beat the pants off your competitors.

NEVER TAKE YES FOR AN ANSWER

Beware of the subtleties of diplomatic speech. Because people don't wish to disappoint or offend, the word "no" is used sparingly in Mexico. But, since unequivocal commitments come sparingly as well, take every "yes" with a grain of salt.

If your Mexican counterpart is unable or unwilling to commit to your proposal, instead of an outright no you are likely to hear some very positive sounding, but noncommittal comments like "Yes, we'd really like to do that."

Sounds pretty good, no? Well, notice that the statement was we'd *like* to do that—not "Yes, we *will* do that."

Your contact may have every intention of eventually closing a deal with you and just isn't quite ready to commit. But then again, without a specific agreement in writing, assume that no agreement has been reached. It's not a matter of honesty or dishonesty, it's a question of manners. Direct confrontation is to be avoided at all costs. Face must always be saved. He wants neither to insult nor to disappoint you.

You have come so far and are wanting or insisting on doing something he may see as impossible or undesirable, and he doesn't want to tell you that (a) he can't or won't do it that way and doesn't want to lose his face; (b) you've wasted your time and money pursuing the impossible and he doesn't want to disappoint you, thereby saving *your* face; (c) he doesn't have any idea what you're talking about, but wants to seem helpful—or any of a dozen other reasons. And, besides, why slam the door now? He may just not be ready to move right now, or maybe he doesn't know you well enough yet. Maybe you can do business in the future.

While this whole attitude can lead to infinite frustration if you are unprepared for it, simple awareness of this trait can forearm you. In negotiations always be *specific*. You can't settle for "soon" as a time frame for action, nor for "this fall," "sometime in October," or even "next week," and certainly not *mañana*. Leave no room for interpretation, specify—Monday, October 1, at 11:00 A.M. If you leave out the details, you are guaranteed changes in your expected arrangements—and *never* do the changes work out in your favor.

As a friend once explained, *mañana* doesn't really mean tomorrow, it just means *not* today.

COMMUNICATIONS—THE FOUR Fs

Repeat after us: fone, fax, FedEx, and *follow up*. Remember these four Fs and you'll limit your communications problems to an absolute minimum.

First phone; discuss what's on your mind personally with your Mexican colleague.

Then fax; after you've resolved matters over the phone, fax a follow-up communiqué recapping your discussion. Request a faxed acknowledgment. Persevere at this until what you have in writing clearly agrees exactly with what you believe was agreed to over the phone.

Then FedEx; whatever materials or document originals are needed to complete the transaction or communication should be air expressed.

Last, but definitely not least, *follow up*! Trust us on this. Whatever "it" is, it won't happen without a firm prod, no matter how good the communications.

Mexico has long suffered from a phone system which would have made a Russian weep. That rare call which did go through was subject to disconnecting in mid-sentence—

or when you finally got it to ring, you discovered that the lines had been crossed and the party that answered was at a totally unrelated number.

These are not isolated cases. Dialing itself requires a maestro's sense of timing and touch. If you dial too fast, the phone steadfastly refuses to respond, not at all unlike a burro unwilling to be prodded into action.

The best you can say about the phone system is that this debilitating handicap has crippled all levels of society equally. One of the authors recounts sitting in the office of one of the most powerful officials in Mexico, who with mounting frustration dialed for half an hour to his home across town for some information. He finally called his secretary in to continue dialing, until the call went through, twenty minutes later. Anyone who has tried to communicate over the phones can spend hours telling horror stories ad nauseam.

Help is allegedly on the way. Southwestern Bell and French Telecom are now joint-venture partners with Telmex and are rumored to be improving the phone system. We say rumored because the results so far have been seen mostly in the stock market, and not on the phone lines.

The *big* change in Mexico's phone system has been the introduction of cellular phones. Most execs (and, indeed, anyone who can afford it) now carry a cellular phone with them at all times. Pay phones are next to useless when you're out of pocket, and it's easier to get a cellular call through than one over the land lines. Hot tip #1: *Get the cellular number of anyone you need to keep in touch with!*

So the first (and often the most difficult) step in business is to reach your Mexican contact by phone. Once you have worked out specific details, *always put it in writing.* The Mexican saying is *Papelito habla*—paper talks. While even in the best of circumstances you can expect delays and changes, without a written agreement, contract, or schedule you must assume that your deal does not exist.

In Mexico you can't assume that anything is done or

agreed to until you can prove it. You can only prove it when you have a document that says so. And the document only says what the document says. Nothing will be extrapolated from the underlying line of thinking that went into its making. No logical conclusions will be drawn.

Be aware that a problem exists if you're having trouble getting the same terms in writing that were discussed over the phone or in person. It may simply be a communications problem or it may be something else. Either way, it's a problem. The fax machine is your savior. Keep faxing back for clarification until you've got it right. *Do not assume* that your Mexican counterpart understands the terms the way you understand them. Get it in black and white before you proceed!

Notice that use of the mail was not included in this discussion on communications. The fax has almost completely replaced the postal service.

Other than bulk-mail type applications, the postal system in Mexico cannot be looked upon as a form of business communication. We send brochures into Mexico and have returns come back to us as much as a year later. The Mexican postal service cannot, in any way, be relied upon to deliver anything in a timely fashion or any fashion at all, for that matter. Lots of mail is just never seen again once it has been posted. This an area that offers great opportunity for improvement in Mexico.

CHAPTER 7

MAJOR MARKETS

No le pido a Dios que me dé,
nomás que me ponga donde hay.

[I don't ask God to give it to me—
just put me where it is.]

Business in Mexico is highly concentrated in its three largest cities: Mexico City, Guadalajara, and Monterrey. Of these three, Mexico City stands alone at the head of the class, with nearly 25 percent of the entire country's population.

MEXICO CITY

You can't really understand Mexico until you've experienced this incredible metropolis, now said to be the world's largest. While its sheer size and mass of humanity are staggering, so too is the concentration of power and wealth.

The current census places the population at eighteen million, while generally accepted estimates place the true figure at over twenty million. For a country of eighty-two million people, this is an incredibly lopsided concentration of population in one city.

As in Washington, D.C., the federal government is concentrated in one area, the Federal District (D.F.), and the city government is one of the nation's most powerful political forces outside of the federal executive.

Obviously, if you are looking to sell consumer goods,

Mexico City is the 800-pound gorilla. More of everything is sold here than in any four or five other cities combined. As with big-city markets everywhere, however, the competition is fierce, and getting the attention of the *chilangos* (as Mexico City residents are not so affectionately referred to throughout the rest of the country) is a monumental challenge.

As in New York or any other major metropolis, the residents of the capital are not easily impressed. They've "seen it all." When dealing business here, be on your toes at all times. The sharks in these waters can be voracious predators. Or worse, they can be so jaded and busy that your "important project" gets put on a back burner while you're all the while being given assurances that everything is moving ahead smoothly. If you start hearing "No te preocupes" (Don't worry about a thing) when you call, start worrying.

By the same token, the rewards of success in this huge market can be overwhelming. If you could sell just one dollar's worth of merchandise to only *five percent* of the people in this city, it would add up to a million dollars in sales. Juggle the numbers however you like—this is a huge market.

By and large you will find the capital's business community to be sophisticated and cosmopolitan. Just as negotiating this city's anarchic traffic requires creativity and total concentration, so too does any attempt at business negotiation. The *chilangos* can demonstrate a degree of complexity, sophistication, and stubbornness rarely seen in business stateside.

Given the immense size of the population, the formidable geographic scale of the city should come as no surprise. Getting from place to place, especially in traffic, can take hours. At the 2:00 P.M. lunch rush even a simple, straight-line jaunt from Reforma down Insurgentes to the upscale business districts of Insurgentes Sur can take anywhere from forty-five minutes to over an hour. God alone can help if you have back-to-back appointments in Satélite, in the North, and Perisur, in the South.

The intersection of Reforma and Insurgentes, distinguished by its statue of the ill-fated Aztec leader Cuauhtémoc, for all practical purposes marks the very center of the city's business life. Most of your appointments are likely to be east or west along Reforma or south down Insurgentes. Your hotel will probably be on Reforma or nearby, in the Zona Rosa, an upscale commercial area that begins at this intersection and forms a wedge to the southwest.

From this starting point, the principal business addresses in town are east along Reforma, to downtown and the Zócalo—where the city government offices, the national palace, and the cathedral are all located; west along Reforma, through the tourist and financial district; Polanco, just north of Reforma at Chapultepec Park; and the Lomas area, up Reforma in the foothills west of Chapultepec; then south, down Insurgentes, particularly Insurgentes Sur, several miles south of the Reforma-Insurgentes intersection; and, holding down the southern end of the city's commercial life, Perisur, with shopping malls and offices.

Heavy manufacturing and distribution are scattered throughout the city, with heavier concentrations north and west of the city center. Naucalpan and Satélite, to the northwest, are noteworthy manufacturing centers.

If you continue west on Reforma, past Chapultepec and Lomas, it eventually becomes the highway to Toluca, capital of the surrounding State of Mexico. Less than an hour's drive from the Polanco neighborhood, Toluca is a heavily industrialized city.

Development between the two cities, somewhat like New York and Newark, is steadily progressing toward one enormous metropolitan area. Plans are already in the works that someday all air-freight traffic currently flying into Mexico City will be diverted to Toluca's airport to make way for increased passenger traffic at Mexico City.

The scale and volume of everything in Mexico City preclude any sort of focus on "core industries." While Monterrey can proudly boast of being the home of the giant industrial groups, many of those same groups' manufacturing facilities are located in and around this vast metropolis. The business of feeding, clothing, and supplying the needs of the twenty million plus inhabitants requires a concentration of industrial resources, which in turn supplies much of the rest of the nation.

If Mexico City has a core industry, it is government. As the capital of a highly centralized government, Mexico City is where the bureaucracy thrives. But, while all government agencies are concentrated there, no attempt has been made to centralize the government's offices within the city. Foreign Relations is in Tlatelolco, off Insurgentes north, the Commerce Department is south of Reforma, near Chapultepec, while the attorney general's office is east, up Reforma past the Alameda Park, and so on.

In an effort at further decentralization, several government agencies have opened satellite offices around the city. So if you have business with the government, be sure you have the right address of the office you're heading for. If you just tell the cab driver to go to the Treasury Department, you could easily wind up at a branch office, miles from where you need to be, wondering what happened.

Quick Traveler's Tips

Mexico's International airport is right in town, an easy twenty- or thirty-minute cab ride to most of the major hotels. Don't accept the offer of a taxi from one of the many cabbies standing right outside the customs area at the airport. Instead, stop at the stand just before entering the baggage inspection area of customs. Here you can buy a taxi ticket at a rate determined by fixed zones. A ticket to the Sheraton, for example, is about $10 U.S. Up to four people can ride to the same destination on one ticket.

Once in the city, there are two kinds of cabs—*sitios*, which operate from a fixed base (often in front of a hotel), are generally bigger, air-conditioned sedans; metered cabs, which roam the streets at random, are usually smaller cars, mostly

Volkswagen beetles with the front passenger seat removed to make more leg-room in the back.

The *sitios* will be considerably more expensive than metered cabs. But if you're part of a group traveling together, or air-conditioning is a priority, it's worth the extra money. You pay a premium for the comfort. It's always a good idea to ask the price to your destination before boarding—once you've arrived, you're in no position to bargain.

Cabs are plentiful all over the city. Because parking is such a problem, cabs are a way of life.

The subway is good, cheap transportation and in many instances can be faster than surface travel. But avoid the rush hours at all costs. Sardines in a can have more elbow room than can be found on the subway at rush hour—to say nothing about the gamy bouquet of a crowded mass of humanity after a hard day's work without air-conditioning. Add pushing and jostling . . .

Mexico City's climate can be confusing—warm in winter and surprisingly cool summer evenings. Our best advice is to take clothing that is neither especially warm nor too light. Be sure to have a sweater or jacket with you in case the evening turns cool, which it can do at any time of the year.

In general, summer is the rainy season. From June through October you should expect an afternoon cloudburst which may or may not finish before sundown. From November through May rain is less likely, but not unheard of. Watch the locals—if they're all carrying umbrellas in the morning, take yours too.

Just for Fun

If you like folk art don't miss the Fonart stores, run by the federal government to provide an outlet for high-quality arts and crafts from throughout the country. There are several in the city. Ask at your hotel's front desk for directions to the one nearest you.

By all means, take a spin through Chapultepec Park, home of several of Mexico City's most visited attractions:

Maximilian's Castle (now the National History Museum); the Museum of Modern Art; and, an absolute must, the world famous National Museum of Anthropology.

We make no pretense about this being a tourist guide to the city. If your schedule allows sufficient time for leisurely exploration, we recommend you get one of the many excellent books written for the pleasure traveler.

MONTERREY

As industry is Monterrey's raison d'être, we'll open our description of this powerhouse with a quote from the excellent Industrial Directory published by CAINTRA, the Chamber of Industry of Nuevo León: "In Monterrey, the industrial Capital of Mexico, the principal cultural values are thrift and hard work."

This simple statement speaks volumes about one of the most industrialized cities on the North American continent and about the sophistication, business acumen, and work ethics of its business leaders. Monterrey's personality today is so totally a product of the huge industrial groups that call it home that to understand the city you first need to know a bit about the distinct structure of the *grupo* as an entity— and then we will treat you to a bit of living group history.

Growth of the *Grupos*

First, let's eliminate a common misconception. Mexican business groups are not like conglomerates, as many U.S. business people inaccurately assume.

Here is why.

The centerpiece of the U.S. conglomerate is a parent company that owns all of its subsidiary enterprises, which are usually related to one industry. These companies rarely share operational techniques or distribution channels. They are basically impersonal and semiautonomous; the ties that bind are a combination of legal stipulations and an annual requirement to contribute their assigned percentage of profits to the parent company.

The Mexican business group, on the *otra mano*, is a mix of seemingly quite diverse companies that flourish in a climate of familial ties, mutual trust, and overall cooperation. The companies often share operating philosophies, channels of distribution, marketing intelligence, and efficiencies of scale seldom exercised in U.S. conglomerates.

Another distinct difference is that nearly every major business group in Mexico has its own source of funds for growth and acquisition in the form of closely held banks and insurance companies. This independent source of ready capital is the balance wheel in the group system. Cash flow surpluses and shortfalls can be balanced among the member companies; the cost of funds is economical and, more important, always there when needed. These strong financial resources also provide group member companies with the wherewithal to strike swiftly when an attractive acquisition or new market opportunity becomes available.

A less public but significant *grupo* strength is the ability and willingness to share key management personnel by temporarily assigning them to assist another member company. This multiple application of high-level expertise offers a ready contingent of corporate smoke jumpers who can immediately respond to a member company's distress signal.

Remember this: when you are attempting to set up a relationship with an established business in Mexico, your product offering and your character may well become the subject of discussion at the next meeting of the business group. It is paramount to your success that both be prepared to survive the group's collective scrutiny.

And now for a bit of living history.

Monterrey, 143 miles south of Laredo, Texas, and 579 miles north of Mexico City, is an incubator for new ideas and entrepreneurial enterprise. It has also been the proving ground for a vanguard of independent Mexican business leaders who disdained languishing behind the traditional safety of government-imposed barriers to foreign trade, in favor of striking out on their own, not only to do business with U.S.- and other foreign-held companies, but to aggressively seek acquisitions outside of Mexico as well.

What is the source of this wellspring of self-confidence that motivates Monterrey business leaders to plow unbroken ground?

The answer, or the beginning of the answer, resides in the business history of two men who joined forces in 1890 to establish a brewery, Cervecería Cuauhtémoc, in Monterrey. Their names were Isaac Garza and Francisco G. Sada, and the business foundation they laid in building their brewery and their vital support for higher education in Monterrey were the cornerstones for almost all of the industry in this city today.

A very real key to their success and one that significantly influenced the emergence of Monterrey as an industrial center is directly related to their visionary approach toward the vertical integration of their companies' products. This approach required enlarged facilities. In turn, the expanded manufacturing capacity provided the opportunity to create new products and accelerate the companies' growth in diversified areas.

As early as 1903, the partners established a plant to manufacture crowns for their bottles and in 1909, when they inaugurated their new glass plant, they began making the bottles as well.

Pressed by World War II, the U.S. in 1942 could no longer be relied on for the steady supply of steel needed for bottle crowns, so the company, by then known as Valores Industriales S.A. or VISA, built a steel foundry; this was followed by a carton manufacturing facility to encase their beer for shipment and a printing facility to provide the millions of labels required for their growing family of brands. In addition to beer and packaging facilities, VISA holdings grew to include a soft drinks division, with brands such as Coca-Cola, Pepsi, and Sprite, a bottled water division featuring Peñafiel and

Bolseca products, and a plant that converts the spent grain used in the brewing process to cattle feed for VISA's beef production operation.

In 1986 Cuauhtémoc brewery acquired Cervecería Moctezuma of Mexico City. The consortium of breweries, now called Cuauhtémoc Moctezuma, produces 50 percent of all beer brewed in Mexico, and its brands are world famous, winning prestigious gold medals at the Munich Oktoberfest time and again. Their leading labels include Bohemia, Carta Blanca, Dos Equis, Superior, and Tecate, as well as a number of regional brands.

VISA currently has twelve companies in what is referred to as the brewery group. Company principals and directors also share major holdings in ALFA, the steel and chemical powerhouse; CYDSA, with its five operating divisions focused on chemicals, fibers, PVC pipe, and water treatment plants; and VITRO, with eight divisions and over one hundred companies manufacturing a huge variety of glass, plastics, stainless steel, and electronic devices for various industrial and consumer applications.

Literate, skilled workers are the bedrock for industrial growth. This vital requirement was recognized and addressed by VISA as well. Under the leadership of Don Eugenio Garza Sada, one of the founder's sons, the Monterrey Institute of Technology was established in 1942 and is today one of the most acclaimed higher education facilities in North America.

The descendants of Isaac Garza and Francisco G. Sada and their extended family members continue to head the boards of directors and manage the leading industrial giants of Monterrey. In typical Monterrey fashion, there has been no reduction in enterprise or productivity with the passing of the generations. In fact, the opposite is true. Each new generation has demonstrated its commitment to both business and social responsibility. This commitment is manifested in the astounding continued growth and expansion of industry and commerce and the ongoing development and cultivation of education and the arts.

In recent years, the old steel mill, an eyesore and environmental nightmare of the first degree, has been transformed into a multiuse complex with a convention center (Cintermex), hotels, theater, sports arena, and recreational water park. In downtown Monterrey, the Marco art museum was opened, with tremendous financial and moral support from the industrial community. In Garza García, the wealthy part of town, ALFA, the largest of the industrial groups, built the Centro Cultural ALFA, a planetarium and natural history museum.

This interconnection of the members of the boards of most of the major companies and the educational and cultural activities of the city was put most clearly to us in a meeting with the chairman of one of Monterrey's largest companies. We were looking to establish an official tie in Monterrey for a civic organization in San Antonio. The business leader suggested that we do it through the board of the chamber of industry. That wasn't exactly the right channel for the contact, so he said why not through the board of the Monterrey Tech—after all, it's the same people. And if not there, the board of the Parque Fundidora might work as well. Again, it's basically the same group, with a different member serving as chairman in each instance, but the connection would be the same.

There are currently eleven universities and over 170 technical and business colleges in Monterrey and the State of Nuevo León, insuring a continuing stream of well-educated and technically skilled employees as well as future entrepreneurs.

With over 7,000 companies involved in over 400 lines of business, there are obviously other extremely successful and powerful entities outside of those previously mentioned; a brief sampling of these includes CEMEX, one of the three largest producers of cement in the world, with ninety-seven concrete and seventeen cement plants throughout Mexico, plus two concrete marketing companies in the U.S. In September 1994 CEMEX purchased a 900,000-metric-ton-per-year production plant in New Braunfels, Texas.

Another major success story involves GAMESA, founded in 1925, as a small baker of cookies, crackers, and biscuits. Dedication to quality control and innovation paid handsome dividends for this well-run company. A merger with Nabisco Famosa of Mexico City in 1981 added other quality products and distribution capabilities to GAMESA. In 1990 PepsiCo, through its Sabritas, S.A. de C.V., subsidiary, bought majority interest in GAMESA. The company has some 14,000 employees working in fourteen plants, and total income has more than tripled in the past five years.

A prime example of Monterrey's ongoing enterprise and industry is Pulsar Internacional, formed in 1986. This rapidly emerging group consists of two divisions, financial and industrial, and employs over 22,000 in Mexico alone, with affiliates and subsidiaries worldwide.

The financial division includes Seguros Comercial América, one of Mexico's largest full-service insurance companies, and Vector, a brokerage and financial services firm. Empresas La Moderna, the industrial division of Pulsar, features Cigarrera La Moderna, with some 60 percent of the tobacco market in Mexico. A companion company, ALUPRINT, and its subsidiary, ELM, produce high-quality, flexible cardboard packaging for the company's internal use as well as supplying many other important international companies such as Kodak, Proctor & Gamble, and Colgate.

At the same time, Pulsar is a major factor in agribusiness around the world. Its BioNova Packing division, acquired in 1993, supplies a major portion of the U.S. west coast with high-quality fresh fruits and vegetables. In November 1994 Empresas La Moderna acquired international seed giant ASGROW from Upjohn for approximately $300 million. This acquisition includes all of ASGROW's worldwide operations, including research, production, and office locations in North America, Europe, and the Pacific Region. In November 1994 Empresas La Moderna also paid approximately $78 million for 57 percent of the outstanding shares of Ponderosa, flagship packaging unit of Empaques Ponderosa.

A final example of the Monterrey influence on innovation and diversification is PROTEXA, a company that began as a small manufacturer of waterproofing products. Currently the company is focused on four areas: petroleum, construction, food and beverage products, and real estate/tourism.

The industry division is made up of twenty companies producing everything from basic construction materials to automotive parts and cellular telephone systems. The construction division is home to seventeen companies and builds offshore drilling platforms and pipelines as well as flying and maintaining fixed wing aircraft and helicopters used in the transport of personnel and materials for industry.

The Tourism and Real Estate division includes nine companies and specializes in building and developing shopping malls, resort hotels, and housing and housing complexes. The Food and Beverage division includes a tuna fishing fleet, a packing plant for tuna, squid, mussels, and sardines; and a vineyard and bottling plant for wines; there are also soft drink bottling plants and distribution services in this completely diversified and well-managed company.

Strong financial underpinning and an understanding of the complexities of various industry financial needs are vital to an industrial economy. With the return of banks to the private sector, Monterrey businesses are well served in this area. With their collective holdings in Bancomer, Banca Serfin, Banca Confia, and Banco de Oriente, over one-half of Mexico's banking assets are controlled by companies and individuals in Monterrey.

With an eye toward decentralization, convenience, and environmental considerations, a number of industrial parks have been developed in and around Monterrey and throughout the state of Nuevo León. Seven of these parks are administered by the state and eight are privately owned. Tax incentives, attractive terms, and other perks are offered to prospective tenants. If you are considering a plant in Mexico, these facilities are certainly worthy of consideration.

Quick Traveler's Tips

Air transportation to and from Monterrey is provided by American, Continental, and the Mexican carriers Mexicana, Aeromexico, Aeromar, and Aero Litoral. The airport is a *long* way out of town—at least forty minutes in light traffic. As in Mexico City, there are authorized cabs for which you can buy a ticket, costing about half what an independent taxi will charge you.

The same cautions apply here as everywhere else in Mexico: don't drive—take a cab or hire a car and driver and arrive on time for your appointments relaxed and ready. Monterrey traffic, like that in any other major city, can be a major headache.

The center of Monterrey is the 100-acre Gran Plaza Square, and on its periphery stand the Central Library, Legislature Palace, Governor's Palace, Mercantile Bank, Cathedral, City Theater, Torre administrative building, and other structures. Downtown is also home of the Hotel Ancira, opening onto Plaza Hidalgo, the Hotel Ambassador just a block away, and a number of excellent restaurants. The majority of business offices tend to be concentrated in the Garza García area, easily accessible by taxi.

Just for Fun

Leave enough time on your business trip to explore Monterrey and the surrounding area. Chipinque Mesa and Horsetail Falls at 5,000 feet are a cool relief from the city streets in the summer. Another interesting attraction is the ALFA Cultural Center in San Pedro Garza García, a science and technology museum built by the ALFA Industrial Group. Other sites to visit include El Obispado (the Bishop's Palace), the Baseball Hall of Fame at the Cuauhtémoc Moctezuma Brewery, and the new Museum of Contemporary Art.

We recommend taking a bit of time to visit some of these attractions—while it's true you are here to do business, it certainly won't hurt if you understand a bit more about the culture. Monterrey is a great business city, and U.S. executives should more readily establish rapport with their counterparts in Monterrey than in any other part of Mexico.

GUADALAJARA

Guadalajara proudly holds the reputation as the most "Mexican" of Mexico's cities. Both the pride and reputation are well founded—nothing could be more Mexican than tequila, mariachis, and charros, the traditional cowboys. Guadalajara is home to each of these cornerstones of Mexican culture.

Weighing in with a population of over four million people, Guadalajara is the commercial and industrial capital of the western coastal region of Mexico. Capital of the State of Jalisco, which is also home to the towns of Tequila and Puerto Vallarta, and thirty minutes by air from Manzanillo and Las Hadas, this is a great business destination.

Guadalajara today weaves together the old and the new. Beautiful colonial buildings stand beside glass and steel structures. Its business community is the most conservative of the three major cities—neither as urbane and coldly "sophisticated" as Mexico City, nor as straightforward and aggressive as Monterrey. But while in this sense too it is the most traditionally Mexican of the big cities, it is also the most charming.

Smog and pollution have become part of the landscape, but not yet to the degree of Mexico City or Monterrey. The climate could hardly be better, with mild-to-warm days and pleasantly cool evenings. Trees line nearly every street and boulevard, and green is definitely the color of the city. A golfer's paradise, Guadalajara has some of the most beautiful courses in North America and the perfect climate for playing year-round.

Guadalajara's population has grown by leaps and bounds in recent years, while its city streets have not. Traffic in the city center can be a snail's crawl if you catch the rush hours and is often frustrating at the best of times.

On a recent business trip, the cab driver was complaining about the traffic, blaming the city's population boom on the hordes of *chilangos* that have moved there from Mexico City since the earthquake in 1985. He said so many had come for the better climate and geological stability that the city's infrastructure just couldn't accommodate them all. Then he started talking about his own family and what a challenge it was to raise *eight* kids as a cab driver, and how his siblings all faced similar difficulties. He was one of seven brothers, who all had followed the big-family tradition. But, of course, all this new traffic *had* to be those interlopers from Mexico City clogging up the works. "Just ten years ago you didn't have these traffic jams . . ."

Guadalajara's commercial and industrial base lacks the intensity and focus of Monterrey or the sheer mass of Mexico City. The business community is more closely knit here than in the other two big cities. As you begin your business you'll find the social "breaking-in" phase may take longer here than elsewhere. Official introductions through government or chamber of commerce ties can be especially valuable ice-breakers.

No one industry or business activity seems to predominate in Guadalajara. While there are certainly powerful individuals and large corporations that call Guadalajara home, their influence and power are not like those exercised by the industrial groups of Monterrey. Grupo Sidek probably stands out as first among peers, with substantial holdings in steel, construction, and resort hotels.

One of Guadalajara's unique claims to fame is its expo and convention center, Expo Guadalajara. For many years the country's only large-scale convention facility, Expo Guadalajara now hosts many of the major trade shows and conventions in Mexico. If you're seeking entree into the market, you should give serious thought to participating in one of the many industry-specific trade shows scheduled throughout the year. Because of Expo Guadalajara's long standing as the country's only facility, the community has developed an efficient infrastructure for servicing shows, and people are accustomed to traveling here to see what's new in their fields.

Quick Traveler's Tips

There's not much different to say here about taxis and drivers. Hire a pro. Downtown is a traffic nightmare. The airport, as in Monterrey, was built with a generous allowance for urban growth—in other words, it's out in the boondocks. Allow yourself at least half an hour travel time to and from.

The hotel zone is a good twenty minutes from downtown, but your business appointments are likely to be out that way as well. Government and retail establishments predominate downtown.

Just for Fun

The "Fiestas de Octubre" began in 1965 and have become one of Mexico's most popular festivities. Each year during the month of October the program includes plays, symphony concerts, flamenco dancers, ballet, sports, contests, and parades. A word of caution—reserve your hotel way in advance.

Some of Mexico's finest arts and crafts are made in Tlaquepaque and Tonalá, suburbs of Guadalajara. Tlaquepaque is a shopper's paradise—colonial buildings, shops piled high with every imaginable type of art and craft, lovely courtyard restaurants, and serious mariachi cantinas and cafes on the town square. Don't miss this side trip!

EVERYWHERE ELSE

Because of the infrastructure problems caused by this immense concentration of business and population in these three cities, the government has undertaken an aggressive program of incentives and regulations to encourage industrial development in other parts of the country. Developing areas that are taking on a new business significance include Puebla, Veracruz, Querétaro, Aguascalientes, Saltillo, Chihuahua, and Hermosillo.

Additionally, the maquiladora industry has had tremendous impact on border cities such as Tijuana, Cd. Juárez, Nuevo Laredo, Reynosa, and Matamoros. As this twin plant industry continues to grow, many new facilities are locating in cities in the interior as well. Guadalajara and Monterrey have both been active and successful in soliciting this welcome foreign investment and development. One big objective of the drive to develop the maquiladora industry in the interior is to provide new jobs and eliminate the need for workers to leave their homes and families in search of employment.

CHAPTER 8

SETTING UP SHOP

*Más vale andar solo
que mal acompañado.*

[It is better to walk alone
than in bad company.]

INBOUND

Importing products from Mexico can be a fascinating and profitable business, but done poorly it can accelerate your physical aging process at the speed of light. You obviously want to enjoy the first and avoid the latter, which, of course, is why you are reading this book!

Finding the products you wish to import is relatively simple. Once you have zeroed in on the product you wish to import, the work really begins. Because it is your economic life on the line, it is vital that you personally meet the owner of the business who will supply your merchandise. You also need to inspect the facilities, examine the products, discuss turnaround time, ask for a list of any other importers they are currently dealing with, and check with them regarding performance and product stability.

Among the points which should be on your inspection checklist are production capacity and existing inventories. One of the most frequently heard complaints among U.S. importers is that the Mexican producer was not able to honor the production requirements or delivery schedules agreed upon.

In many cases this stems from vast differences in the market structures between the two countries. A major retailer who wants to buy dinettes from a Mexican producer may need 10,000 units a month. The manufacturer may make outstanding quality dinettes, but the most ever produced in a month was 200 units. This obviously leads to problems for both parties.

Once you are satisfied that a deal can be made, then it is time to structure a *written* agreement. Remember the Mexican caveat in Chapter 6: *papelito habla*—paper talks, and they said it first! In fact this would be a good time to reread that chapter. Your adherence to the rules in those few pages can spell the difference between a productive relationship and the dreaded speed-of-light aging process we mentioned above. Our recommendation is that you engage a U.S. law firm with real-world experience in Mexican contract law, which also has a relationship with a Mexican firm skilled in the same area.

Import Assistance

We are often asked about U.S. government assistance programs available for imports. To put it simply—they don't exist. The U.S. government views its role as promoting exports, thus helping to balance our international trade.

A great resource for the importer is the Foreign Trade Bank of Mexico, Bancomext. It has representative offices all over the U.S. The representative is known as the trade commissioner of Mexico. Bancomext offers trade leads and export financing for Mexican exporters and importers of Mexican products abroad. In most cities where there is both a trade commission and a consulate, the commissioner plays the role of commercial attaché, with full diplomatic status.

In addition, many of Mexico's states have trade offices in the U.S. set up to facilitate investment in their area or to generate export opportunities for their products. These offices can assist by providing direct contact with specific product manufacturers as well.

Contact information for Mexican consulates in North America is listed in Appendix IV.

Outbound

The question we get asked most often is "How do I distribute my products in Mexico?" The simple answer is that your distribution options there are very much the same as they are in the U.S. But wait a minute . . . don't run off quite yet. While the answer really is pretty simple, there are some complex logistical twists that need explanation.

Mexico is no different than anywhere else when it comes to "legally binding" arrangements. Contracts are only as good as the parties signing them. Look at the complications and expenses involved in enforcing a contract on your own home turf in the U.S—then multiply those by a factor of 100 when trying to enforce terms on an uncooperative party in a foreign country, under a very different civil and penal code. What's more, you are on your *adversary's* home turf—I think you get the picture.

We have two pieces of advice regarding any of the following distribution arrangements:

1. Think Mexican. Take the time to get to know the people personally. Observe their business operation and talk to their customers and, if possible, their competitors. If anything makes you uncomfortable about them, dig deeper or look for someone else. Don't jump in bed with the first candidate that comes along promising the moon. As an old carpenter friend said, measure twice, cut once.

2. Get a good lawyer who's well versed in both U.S. and Mexican law to draw up the agreement. You want the terms to be enforceable in both countries.

Direct Sales

Starting with the basics, you do have some specific options in your approach to distribution. You or a salesperson from your organization can sell directly to the Mexican clients. This involves considerable expense in travel and maintenance costs. When problems arise, you may have to appear personally to solve them, incurring travel expenses and lost time.

The obvious advantage of this method is that you maintain complete control over the operation, establish personal rapport with your clients, and retain all of the profits. Among the many down sides are the elevated costs and the fact that you're not there on a day-to-day basis to care for the business and, unless you warehouse products at a public facility in Mexico (not recommended), every order has to be shipped internationally, causing delays in shipping and receipt. Also, embarking upon this method of sales means you're starting from scratch on every account. Results could be agonizingly slow in coming.

Branch Office

If you're ready to make a more serious commitment to the market, you may want to look at opening a branch office in Mexico.

This structure allows you to have U.S. personnel working in Mexico. There is no Mexican tax on the income of these personnel as long as the company's U.S. office is paying their taxes in the United States. The stipulation is that these employees can only work in Mexico for 183 days during a twelve-month period. In the event that the employees continue to work in Mexico past this period, they will receive exemptions or lower tax rates on the first $80,000 U.S. earned.

Branch operations or subsidiaries must apply for a federal registration number just as Mexican companies are required to do. Your company is subject to taxes at the same

level as Mexican companies; however, no additional tax
will be imposed on income already subject to corporate tax.
There are no restrictions on the remission of royalties, dividends, honorariums, or other types of payment to foreign
workers in Mexico.

Obviously you can also employ Mexican workers in a
branch office if you prefer. Here again you should seek expert
legal assistance, as the laws concerning compensation, benefits, and in particular the costs associated with discharging
or laying off a Mexican employee are quite different than
those in the U.S.

Broker/Representative

The third approach is hiring a broker or representative. Find
someone already selling complementary but noncompetitive
products to your target clientele. To find your best prospects,
start by calling potential clients (found in the yellow pages):
ask who's calling on them and who they would recommend
as a rep. Other good sources of leads are trade shows, chambers of commerce, and the U.S. Department of Commerce,
which has officers in the embassy in Mexico City and in
many of the consulates throughout the country.

In most cases a few names will come up repeatedly.
Through an interview process, you should be able to select
one from this candidate list. Determine what geographical
areas you want to assign by where the representative's
strengths are.

Several questions need to be resolved at the very beginning. Inventory and warehousing—will stock be maintained
locally? Under what conditions? Who pays for storage, shipping, and handling? Promotional expenses—what will you
provide? What is expected of the representative? Pricing policy, terms of sale, and credit and collections—what is your
policy? What is the market norm? In which currency will
payments be made? Duration of agreement—what span of
time does the agreement cover? Under what circumstances

can it be terminated? Territories—what is the representative's territory? Will he or she be your exclusive rep within that territory?

Finally, recap what you've discussed—what your expectations of each other are and what you understand each other's responsibilities to be—then commit it all to paper. Remember, *papelito habla*—paper talks. Never assume from your discussions that you understand each other. Spell out every detail. This is just good business anywhere, but for some reason these details seem to get overlooked in the excitement of closing a deal in Mexico.

Master Distributor

Another way of achieving your distribution goals is to establish a master distributor, either by region or for the entire country. Once established, your master distributor becomes your only direct customer in that territory. All merchandise is shipped to one warehouse (unless arrangements are made for drop shipments to clients), and the distributor is then responsible for individual sales within the territory. Generally, in this kind of relationship, the master distributor maintains local inventory and sells to retail dealers within the territory.

The advantages are many. You only have one client to deal with, and only one address to ship to. Larger, consolidated shipments offer economies of scale, especially over long distances and over borders. Your recordkeeping is greatly simplified, and your costs are minimized. For many companies, this is the most efficient and cost-effective means of managing distribution in Mexico.

But, as great as the advantages can be if all goes well, the disadvantages can be equally great if there are problems. First and foremost, you have placed all of your eggs in one basket. If your master distributor doesn't perform, you're out of business. Great care must be made in drawing up the distributor agreement, specifying performance standards that must be met. Otherwise, you could find yourself contractually locked into a dead-end relationship. Depending on how your distribution contract is written, you may have great difficulty "firing" your distributor.

Another disadvantage of this kind of relationship is the fact that you have no direct control over the market. You are completely reliant upon someone else to represent you and sell for you. You have little or no contact with the end-users of your products.

This, though, can be remedied to some extent by designing programs of sales support for your distributor where you send in your own account sales reps or factory reps to call on end-users for account maintenance or customer relations. Not only is it good sales and public relations to do so, but you should always be prepared for the potential of having your master distributor jump ship and take on a competitor's line. If you've had no contact with the customers, you could be in big trouble.

Joint Venture

Saving the best for last, one very effective relationship you should consider is to enter into a joint venture with a Mexican partner. With the positive changes in the Foreign Investment Act, this has become very attractive and, properly structured, offers great advantages.

As joint venture partners, both sides contribute something of value from the very beginning. Whether it's investment money, product, established distribution, technical expertise, or something else, the idea is that both sides contribute and therefore have a vested interest in the success of the business and share proportionally in the proceeds.

Joint ventures can be formed to carry out virtually any type of business activity—from heavy manufacturing to simple sales and marketing.

While the joint venture approach has its share of pitfalls, you can at least expect that with shared ownership the degree of attention paid to the business at hand will be greater under this arrangement than is likely under any other. Be prepared to commit yourself to painstaking research on the background of candidates for this important alliance.

Immigration and Visas

On your initial exploratory visits to Mexico, you can use the basic tourist visa issued by the airlines or travel agent. This is good for a single entry into the country, with a maximum stay of 180 days. As part of NAFTA's implementation, a simple thirty-day business visa, called a FMN, was created for U.S. and Canadian citizens.

Once you begin traveling in and out of Mexico on a regular basis for business, you will want to get a nonimmigrant work visa, known as an FM3. This is good for one year at a time and allows unlimited entries and exits. You can apply for this work visa at the nearest Mexican embassy or consulate or, as a last resort, with the Secretaría de Gobernación in Mexico. (If you've never had the pleasure of dealing with the federal bureaucracy in Mexico, take our recommendation and deal with the embassy or consulate in the U.S.)

BUSINESS STRUCTURES IN MEXICO

There are a variety of corporate structures available under Mexican law and as in the U.S. they are designed to serve specific business needs. Here is a brief description of some of them and a definition of the abbreviations used in company names.

The most frequently seen symbol is S.A., which stands for Sociedad Anónima or its U.S. counterpart, the famous "Inc."; both mean that the company is a corporation—period. Others are:

S.A. de C.V., Sociedad Anónima de Capital Variable or a corporation with variable capital. Both S.A. and S.A. de C.V. are commonly used by both domestic and foreign investors.

S. de R.L., Sociedad de Responsabilidad Limitada or limited liability company.

S. en C., Sociedad en Comandita. A limited partnership, rarely used.

S.C., Sociedad Civil. Civil partnership of a noncommercial nature used by professional practitioners, educational units, etc.

S. en N.C., Sociedad en Nombre Colectivo. A general partnership sometimes used by foreign investors to qualify as a foreign partnership in their own country. Unlimited liability.

A.C., Asociación Civil or Civil Association, primarily applied to not-for-profit or charitable organizations.

A. en P., Asociación en Participación, the previously mentioned joint venture contract.

E. de P.F., Empresa de Persona Física, a sole proprietorship, not available to foreigners.

S. de S. E., Sucursal de Sociedad Extranjera or branch of a foreign corporation.

Recent Changes in Mexican Corporate Law

Mexican laws pertaining to corporations and limited partnerships have recently been revised. Corporations or Sociedades Anónimas may now be formed with as few as two shareholders (the previous requirement specified a minimum of five shareholders). Limited partnerships or Sociedades de Responsabilidad Limitada may now include as many as fifty partners.

These two changes are significant. First, the incorporation revision eliminates the problems associated with having five shareholders in a small start-up corporation. Second, the expansion allowing up to fifty participants in a limited partnership spreads the risk and reduces amount of cash required of each investor for projects with substantial capital requirements.

Foreign Investment in a Nutshell

The rules governing foreign investment and ownership of business in Mexico were substantially revised by the Salinas administration to encourage economic growth. The changes are a dramatic contrast to the rigid protectionism that had been the standard since the revolution and are intended to increase industrial production, enhance growth and stability in the work force, and generate a larger export base.

As part of the process of change, the National Institute of Statistics, Geography, and Data prepared the Mexican Classification of Economic Activities and Products that identifies those that are classified and require prior approval from the Commission on Foreign Investment.

The classified activities list is divided into categories:

CATEGORY 1. Activities considered to be "strategic," reserved exclusively for the state. Examples: Oil and gas production and the primary petrochemical industry.

CATEGORY 2. Activities reserved exclusively for Mexican nationals. Examples: Television and radio broadcasting.

CATEGORY 3. Activities where foreign investment is limited to 34 percent foreign ownership. Examples: Mining and/or refining iron ore.

CATEGORY 4. Activities where foreign investment is limited to 40 percent. Examples: Secondary petrochemical products and the automotive parts industry.

CATEGORY 5. Activities where foreign investment is limited to 49 percent. Examples: Mining and refining precious and metallic ores.

CATEGORY 6. Activities where prior approval is required if foreign ownership is to exceed 49 percent. Examples: The construction industry, accounting and legal services.

As you can see, the classified categories are relatively limited, which opens a huge number of previously restricted activities for foreign investment and ownership without the necessity of seeking prior authorization simply by complying with the following requirements.

1. The initial investment in fixed assets during the preoperating stage may not exceed U.S. $100 million. Larger investments will probably be authorized, but prospective investors must inform the authorities about them to make sure all the necessary infrastructure is available.

2. The investment must consist of foreign funds. One exception is for investments made by foreign investors already established in Mexico. They may use funds held in Mexico. Shareholders' equity must equal at least 20 percent of the investment in fixed assets at the end of the initial start-up stage.

3. The industrial or manufacturing facilities of new companies must be located outside zones designated as high-density industrial areas: Mexico City, the cities of Monterrey and Guadalajara, and certain municipalities in the State of Hidalgo and municipalities in the State of Mexico belonging to Zone III-A, known as Controlled Growth Areas and listed in a decree issued on January 22, 1986.

4. Companies must maintain an overall favorable foreign exchange balance during the first three years of operation.

5. Permanent jobs must be created as a consequence of the new investment. Companies must establish continuing

training and education programs to promote employee skills and development.

In considering the authorization of foreign investment exceeding 49 percent in classified categories the commission on Foreign Investment uses certain basic criteria:

1. Will the proposed investment complement the domestic investment?

2. Will the investment support a positive balance of payments and promote exports?

3. Will the investment create jobs and enhance employee earnings?

4. Will the investment contribute to the development of zones or regions where economic improvement is a high priority?

5. Will the investment bring in new technology and contribute to the development of local technological research?

Approval Process   The approval process for any foreign investor includes prior authorization of the Ministry of Foreign Affairs for every type of corporation or other business entity. Authorization may also be required from the National Commission on Foreign Investment. All companies partially or wholly owned by foreigners must register with this commission.

When all required governmental authorizations have been acquired, the business entity's charter and bylaws must be formalized in a public deed executed before a notary public.

Legal Assistance   Obviously any foreign investor should engage a qualified law firm to draw up business documents. Our recommendation is to hire an American firm familiar with Mexican law to assist you in establishing contact with qualified and reliable Mexican law firms. As in all business, there are sharks aplenty in the legal profession, who prey upon the unwary foreigner.

Be sure that the counsel you hire *really* has experience in Mexico. You need someone to tell you whether the permits you're being told you need are indeed required or just a make-work job to pad some local attorney's pocket. You may never know how much your U.S. law firm saved you—until you hear someone else's expensive tale of woe.

Expeditious Processing of Applications   In order to streamline the bureaucratic process, the Salinas administration decreed that all applications for foreign investment permits be decided upon within forty-five working days. If no response is forthcoming within that period, the application is automatically approved.

Don't assume that this means a free ride. On the contrary, this has produced a significant reduction in response time from formerly torpid and unmotivated bureaucrats. You should expect a decision regarding your application within the allotted time.

Wouldn't it be refreshing if our own government would adopt a similar incentive to jump-start our "public servants" into action?

Taxes and Incentives

1.   Corporate earnings are taxed only once at 35 percent.

2.   All inventory investment may be deducted immediately upon purchase for corporate income tax purposes as opposed to making a future deduction for the cost of goods sold.

3.   Investors have an option to write off a substantial portion of newly acquired fixed assets. This option does not apply to assets used in the Federal District,

Guadalajara, or Monterrey due to the government's decentralization policy designed to spread economic growth more evenly. Note: many other states and cities in Mexico now offer attractive incentives for the establishment of new industries.

4. Components or raw material used in the manufacture of export goods may be imported into Mexico duty-free.

5. Export goods are assigned a zero rate of value added tax (VAT). Exporters can obtain refunds of VAT charged by any of their suppliers as well.

6. Duty-free import zones exist. There are no foreign trade zones.

Financing and Assistance   Local venture capital is available for a variety of businesses, with the preference being export-oriented industries. As a matter of fact, preferential notes are available on loans dedicated to export goods.

Privatization of the banking system, the return of Mexican capital, and improved government financing will no doubt deepen the pool of investment capital.

The U.S. government has several programs to aid exporters of American-made products. Agencies such as the U.S. Department of Commerce, through its Foreign and Commercial Service, the Trade and Development Agency, the Export-Import Bank, and others have programs for the exporter.

In all honesty, we have never known of any *small* businesses which have directly benefited from these programs. Most require a degree of skill in maneuvering through the bureaucratic maze which is beyond the resources and scope of the majority of small businesses.

International development organizations in cooperation with Mexican banks are providing financing at preferential rates for the importation of machinery and equipment for new or expanding businesses.

Remittance of Capital and Profits   Capital may be repatriated without restriction, and there are no exchange controls or restrictions on the payment of profits. This applies to both initial and subsequent investments. The payment of technical assistance fees, royalties, or stock dividends to nonresidents is not subject to exchange controls. As long as payments are made from prior earnings, dividends can be paid without limitation.

Fiscal Year   The calendar year is the legal fiscal year and applies to all tax issues.

Real Estate Investment/Border and Coastal Areas   The foreign investment regulations authorize the establishment of renewable thirty-year trusts for foreigners who wish to hold and use real estate for industry or tourism purposes within 100 kilometers (62 miles) from the border or 50 kilometers (31 miles) from the coastline.

Maquiladoras   Enhanced processing companies or maquiladoras are Mexican corporations that can be wholly owned by a foreign corporation with which they have a contract to produce subassemblies, assemblies, or finished goods for shipment to the foreign company.

The foreign company furnishes machinery, equipment and materials, or parts to be assembled or processed. All is imported duty free, under bond, into Mexico and remains the property of the foreign corporation. The Mexican company supplies the building and labor required to produce the goods and in return recapture its actual costs plus a modest profit.

In a typical arrangement, a U.S. company sets up a maquiladora to take advantage of the much lower manual labor costs in Mexico. The basic materials are manufactured at the company's plants in the U.S. and shipped in bond to the maquiladora in Mexico, where labor-intensive processes are carried out. These may include some further processing of the original manufactured items or assembly of component subassemblies.

For instance, an electronics manufacturer may make the chips and chassis of its product in the U.S. and ship the unassembled pieces to the maquiladora, where these components are assembled. The assembled, finished product is then returned to the United States, where it is assessed customs duties only on the value of the labor performed.

When the maquiladora concept began in the 1960s, most of the "twin plant" operations were located close to each other, on opposite sides of the border. This geographic tie no longer restricts the industry. Today there are maquiladoras in and around many of the major cities of Mexico's interior. Components are shipped in from all over the U.S., with the final product often destined for sales around the world.

From the program's inception, Mexican law required that the vast majority of the output of a maquiladora be exported. With the continued opening of the economy, maquiladoras are now being allowed to sell a larger share of this output in Mexico.

Patents, Trademarks, Copyrights

The Law for the Development and Protection of Industrial Property became effective on June 28, 1991, replacing the former Patent and Trademark Law. The Copyright Law was amended on August 18, 1991. Recent amendments provide additional safeguards that afford protection on a par with the world's most industrialized nations.

Patents are now issued for a nonextendable term of twenty years.

Trademarks can be registered for renewable ten-year terms indefinitely.

Copyright protection is granted for a term of fifty years upon determination of ownership of rights and registration with the Copyright Department of Ministry of Public Education (Dirección de Derechos de Autor).

CHAPTER 9

SHIPPING LOGISTICS

Lo barato es caro.

[What's cheap is expensive.]

If your interest in Mexico includes importing or exporting merchandise, then you will sooner or later be faced with decisions regarding transportation and documentation and how the heck do you get your stuff over the border? The normally simple act of shipping from point *A* to point *B* seems to take on Byzantine complications when there's an international border in between.

The only comprehensive source for detailed information regarding import and/or export permits, licenses, customs duties, etc., is the customs house broker. They are the professionals who dedicate their working lives to these matters. Our intent is to give you an overview of the system and a general look at how goods flow across the border, both north and south.

As a result of our 2,000 miles of shared border, the vast majority of all freight between Mexico and the U.S. travels by truck or rail.

There is a logistical difference between shipping a product to Europe and shipping that same product to Mexico. When you load your cargo on a ship for export, you prepare the documents in advance and can even send them in

advance to the customs broker on the other side of the At-
lantic, so that he or she can begin preclearance before the
shipment arrives. You know that the transit time is measured in days or weeks and are prepared mentally for it.

A different mindset is at work on shipments to or from
Mexico. If you're shipping by container, it doesn't seem
much different than any other shipment that leaves your
dock. "Why does it always seem to get hung up at the border? After all, when I ship to or receive shipments from
Japan or Europe, there's no delay en route."

The difference is the border. It's not at the beginning or
end of the journey. It's right smack in the middle. The bureaucratic delay isn't where you can see it or understand it.
It's out in some "godforsaken desert frontier town in the
middle of nowhere."

That's certainly not an accurate description of the border, but it *is* the mental image many people hold of it. How
many people who ship goods through Laredo, or El Paso, or
Nogales have ever actually been there?

There's an air of mystery and intrigue that surrounds the
activities of customs and freight handling on the border. To
a great extent, this is no accident. The less you understand
about what you're paying for, the more you'll end up paying
for it.

This section does not pretend to be a complete guide to
shipping and transportation, but rather a basic primer to remove some of the mystery from the procedure. Let's start in
the middle—the border—and then work our way back there
from both ends.

In order to import into Mexico any commercial shipment of $1,000 or more, you must employ the services of
a licensed Mexican customs house broker, whose job is to
handle the documentation and to physically bring the freight
over the border. It is essential to understand what the customs broker does in order to be in a position to negotiate the
best rates and services for your situation.

There are four official roles that customs brokers play on the U.S.-Mexico border. On southbound shipments they fill out the U.S. export declaration and the Mexican import documents. Northbound they fill out the Mexican export and the U.S. import documents. In making the customs declarations for importing goods into either country, it is their responsibility to accurately declare the nature and origin of the product and to pay all corresponding duties and taxes.

Of those four activities, three are carried out by the Mexican broker and only one by the U.S. broker. Southbound the Mexican brokers do everything. They file the very simple U.S. export declaration, which, unless the merchandise is a restricted commodity, is only for Department of Commerce tracking purposes. They then handle the Mexican import documentation and customs declaration.

The one role that a U.S. customs broker can fill for you on southbound shipments is that of your agent, receiving and holding the cargo in a yard until the Mexican agent has inspected it and payment is made. As you can see, this is no small role! If you sell your product FOB mid-bridge, then you need to establish a relationship with a good U.S. broker.

On northbound shipments, the Mexican broker handles the export filing on the Mexican side, and the U.S. broker receives the goods and files the U.S. customs declaration and import documents.

This is an extremely important detail. The amount of customs duty you pay depends on how they classify and declare your shipment. If you're going to be shipping regularly, a little research on this in advance can save you big bucks over the long run. There may be more than one way to describe the same article for customs purposes, and different duties may apply depending on those descriptions.

SOUTHBOUND

Now, what are the actual mechanics of a shipment going into Mexico from the U.S.? In the most common scenario, the American shipper sells a product FOB mid-bridge, some-where on the border. It is shipped to a warehouse on the U.S. side of the border, where the shipment must be offloaded and inspected by the Mexican customs broker. Mexican customs places the burden of compliance on the broker, who must unload the container and verify its contents, the quantities, and, if applicable, the serial numbers of the items. This is obviously a laborious task, but unavoidable.

Once the contents have been verified, the broker acknowledges to the recipient in Mexico that the goods are in order, and the transaction is consummated. In this type of situation, payment is usually made at this point by a letter of credit or other means arranged between the parties.

The broker then submits the documentation to Mexican customs for processing; the shipment is crossed, duties are paid, and onward into Mexico it goes.

This seems simple enough, and really, in most cases, it should be. But horror stories abound of how shipments have taken days, weeks, or even months, and cost small fortunes, to clear customs and cross the border. What happens?

Many factors can enter into the equation. Simple logistics snafus and poor service account for many of the problems we've seen. At Laredo, one of the busiest border crossings in the world, thousands of trucks cross each day. This puts such a heavy demand on the brokers there that you have to select carefully to find one who is capable and willing to provide you with the service you need.

Under normal circumstances, the actual clearance of the documents through customs should take no more than twenty-four hours. It's in the preparation of those documents that the delays usually come.

Remember, they have to unload each container and verify its cargo before forwarding it into Mexico. When they're backed up with other traffic, you may get bumped down the priority list. If there's a problem rectifying quantities or descriptions of merchandise with the actual contents, that can cause substantial delays. On the Mexican end, if an import permit is required for the merchandise in question, you'd better be sure that it has been arranged in advance of the arrival of the shipment.

While the permit issue is specifically of concern to the Mexican side of the border and therefore, if you're selling FOB mid-bridge, is not technically your concern, good customer relations dictate that you check with your client in Mexico before shipment to assure that this has been addressed.

A broker friend told of a shipment going into Mexico that (fortunately for the seller) was sold FOB mid-bridge, Laredo. The broker received the product at his warehouse on the U.S. side and called the Mexican broker appointed by the recipient, who examined the load and verified to the Mexican client its contents. Our broker friend received payment on behalf of the U.S. shipper; at that point, the product became the property of the Mexican client. The Mexican broker then began processing the documentation for import into Mexico. It turned out that the product in question required a special import permit, which the client did not have.

To make a long story short, it took six months to arrange the permit, throughout all of which time the cargo sat in the yard of our friend, the U.S. broker, accruing storage and handling charges. The shipper was paid on time and both brokers made a killing on the deal, but the buyer really got nailed—all because he failed to do his homework prior to placing the order.

With the normalization of business practices between our countries, more and more products are being sold FOB-destination. A number of freight lines now offer door-to-door service. This makes it more important than ever to understand the procedures at the border. Traditionally, the attitude has been, "I'll get it *to* the border. From there on, it's your problem." Shippers on this side didn't want to know what went on in the crossing process. But if you take the time to figure out the game, you can now offer delivered prices and complete service to clients in Mexico that can set you apart from your competition.

It will help to know some background on Mexican customs brokers. This is an *extremely* profitable business in Mexico. Not only is the client billed for all duties and taxes assessed by the government, but the brokers charge a fee based on a percentage of the value of the shipment. Then they add on service charges for unloading and reloading the container, phone calls and faxes (often whether there were any or not), correspondence, etc. By the time they've tagged on all of their charges their fee may run over $1,000 per container. Figure that the bigger brokers in Laredo may cross fifty trucks or more every day, and you begin to see what a gold mine this is.

It can be very difficult to get a definitive estimate of brokering charges in advance. If you get the feeling at times that there is a conspiracy of obfuscation, you are not necessarily paranoid. The less you understand, the more you'll get charged.

Customs brokering licenses in Mexico have long been granted in reward for political favors. At the end of a president's term he would offer to his inner circle their choice of government-granted licenses. A customs broker's license has always been one of the most sought after political rewards.

In keeping with his program of cleaning up the traditional system of official patronage, President Salinas, upon taking office, declared that all those who had received new licenses within the prior eighteen months would have to re-qualify by taking the exams over again. If they passed they could keep their license. This succeeded in weeding out some of the most blatant cases of cronyism. And, with the changes in the market overall, a new breed of customs broker is emerging: direct, open, and all business.

To protect yourself, you should insist on a clear estimate of charges prior to shipment. Demand to be notified of any additional charges before they are incurred so that you have the option of approving them or not. If you feel that you're getting the runaround, say so, and shop until you get what you want. Shop prices. Freight from the border to Mexico City can vary from as much as $1,500 to as little as $900 on the same shipment. Customs brokering charges on the same shipment can vary as much as 100 percent. Don't assume or accept the argument that there are "standard rates." Someday soon there may be, but it certainly hasn't happened yet.

NORTHBOUND

The routine for northbound shipments out of Mexico into the United States is made somewhat simpler by the fact that U.S. customs has traditionally put the burden of compliance on the shipper and not on the customs broker. Once a shipment has been cleared for export by the Mexican broker, the import documentation is turned over to the U.S. broker for product classification, etc. As opposed to their Mexican counterparts, the U.S. brokers do not have to unload the shipment and verify every aspect of the invoice and documentation.

U.S. customs accepts the commercial invoice and bill of lading at face value and does not (usually) hold the broker liable for errors. Based on the shipping documents, the broker classifies the merchandise for customs purposes and makes the import declaration. If the shippers erred in stating the contents, the penalties are levied against them. This speeds up the process considerably.

When expecting a shipment from Mexico, you can save a considerable amount of time by having the shipper fax you a copy of the packing list and the invoice. With these documents in hand, your U.S. customs broker can submit documentation to U.S. customs in advance of receipt for preclearance. Almost all U.S. brokers are connected on-line to the U.S. Customs computer system, and the processing is done electronically.

Because of the uniformity of access and controls inherent in the U.S. Customs procedures, it is much easier to get a clear and accurate estimate of duties and charges prior to entering into a transaction. If you're planning to import products from Mexico, set up a relationship with an experienced customs broker before you make your first buying trip. This can save you enormous amounts of time and heartache.

Ask about both duties and restrictions. Those beautiful wool sweaters are fairly easy to import, but if they contain *any* acrylic fiber content, you must have a special visa to bring them in. There are a number of such restrictions that you would do well to know before you get your heart set on bringing in a container-load of some item.

It's not enough to find a good product at a good price. You have to be able to get it to where you can sell or use it within a reasonable amount of time, and without disastrous unforeseen costs being added on. This may sound elementary, but the brokers tell us that this painful lesson is learned the hard way every day by unprepared clients.

SHIPPING OPTIONS

There are many methods of shipping both to and from Mexico and numerous factors to take into consideration in selecting the one most suited to your product, imported or exported. The options for shipping into or out of Mexico are essentially equal to those in the U.S. Mexico's major cities are served by air, rail, truck, and on the Pacific and Gulf coasts by ship.

In deciding how best to ship your merchandise into or out of Mexico, certain standard guidelines should be adhered to. Large heavy freight, such as factory equipment, may be cheaper to send by ship to the port nearest the final destination and then sent on by rail or truck. The advantage is cost; the disadvantages are variable scheduling and slowness of arrival.

If the product has great value or must meet a deadline, air may be the only option. The advantage is speed. The disadvantage may be cost. The value, size, and nature of your merchandise will determine how you sell and ship your products.

TERMS OF THE TRADE

FOB: Free on Board	Seller will deliver goods to shipper, but freight charges are borne by buyer.
FAS: Free alongside Ship	Seller will deliver goods to ship. Buyer pays for transportation costs from there forward.
CNF: Cost of Goods & Freight	Sales contract that includes goods and shipping costs.
CIF: Cost of Insurance & Freight	Price quoted in shipping contract includes cost of freight and insurance.

Factors to Consider

- Just-in-time inventory control: This growing trend is designed to free up working capital and diminish the usually top-heavy inventory to sales ratio. Shipping choice—proven, reliable truck line or airfreight.

- Containerization: A variety of merchandise can be loaded in containers at factory with a single bill of lading.

- Bonded area: International shipments can be quickly sorted and cleared through customs. This provides timely access for customs and brokerage staff to open, inspect, review documentation, and reseal the cargo for delivery to its final destination.

- Bonded warehousing: Merchandise can be stored duty-free and tax deferred for up to five years.

- Foreign trade zone: Allows goods and components to be stored duty-free and provides facilities for assembly and repair work before goods are sold.

- Parts bank: Certain airfreight companies provide 24-hour-a-day access to merchandise held in their parts bank, where they both store and distribute merchandise for the shipper or manufacturer.

Hidden Expenses

The following expenses are often overlooked. Be sure to factor them into your shipping budget.

- Cost of document preparation by broker, shipper

- Insurance costs for loss, damage, theft, length of time in transit

- Packing costs for different shipping methods

- Local pickup and delivery costs

- Inland haul to airport or port gateway

- Carrier charges, port of exit, port of arrival

- Surcharges and valuation

- Landing and broker's fees at port of arrival

- Transportation and warehouse costs from factory to customer

- Interest charges on idle capital

- Inventory carrying cost

CHAPTER 10

ADVERTISING IN MEXICO

El que no enseña no vende.

[You won't sell what you don't show.]

The cost of success in advertising in Mexico is eternal vigilance, and even then it probably won't go smoothly. Along with nearly every other facet of business there, virtually the entire spectrum of print and broadcast media is undergoing transition. Competition is beginning to raise its lovely little head and bringing with it a heretofore unfelt need to provide a modicum of reliable service.

This doesn't mean that your ads will be placed when and where you contracted and paid. It's just that now you can find the odd soul who will agree with you that your account wasn't handled properly.

No doubt you're now asking yourself what the heck we're rambling on about. Well, it goes like this: in consultation with your ad agency, you carefully map out a schedule for a series of ads to appear in the largest, most prestigious newspaper in your target market. You contract and prepay for ads to appear. On day one of your campaign the ad is mysteriously absent.

After a hundred dollars' worth of phone calls back and forth to the agency, everyone agrees that the paper screwed up, but that the ad will appear *without fail* tomorrow. And so it does, probably with special placement to placate you.

If luck is with you, this injection of adrenaline early in the relationship may be sufficient to keep the newspaper and/or ad agency on the straight and narrow. But don't count on it. We've had ads run without incident for weeks at a time and then fail to show on the opening day of the event they're advertising—always with heartfelt apologies and promises to make up the shortfall by superior placement and/or double ads the next day, and maybe even special editorial coverage.

Your best defense is to hire a good ad agency and only pay partially in advance. Then at least you retain some leverage to insure that every effort is made on your behalf. If not, threaten to withhold payment. It's no guarantee, nor does it remedy the loss from a critical missing ad, but it's the best pressure you've got.

Television is just as bad. A classic scenario if you're placing nationwide advertising, either on TV or in the newspapers, is that the ad will appear as scheduled, but only in Mexico City. The rest of the country is somehow skipped. Maybe it's an oversight, maybe they just figured you wouldn't notice.

If at all possible, cover yourself by having someone in each of the markets where your ad is scheduled to appear either buy the paper or record the program in which the ad should be. This may be your only proof of insertion or failure to perform. We and many of our associates have unsuccessfully argued that an ad failed to appear as scheduled, until we provided hard evidence—the Guadalajara edition of the paper or a videocassette of the program, recorded in Aguascalientes. Only then is it reluctantly admitted that this may indeed have happened, but "you don't understand, this is Mexico, and it happens all the time, don't get so upset . . ."

The one exception we have found to this rule has been *El Norte*, the leading paper of Monterrey and without question the most professional news organization in Mexico.

So much for the bad news. The good news is that you have some very attractive advertising options in Mexico that you can't get in the United States. Not only can you purchase "ad" space, you can also buy "editorial coverage." In fact, in some instances, the only way to get editorial coverage of your event or product is to pay for it. This may raise the hackles of the press community in the U.S., but as a marketing person, it's nice to know you can guarantee the editorial coverage of your choice.

With the notable exception of *El Norte*, editorial coverage on any subject can be bought for the right price in virtually any newspaper in Mexico. Far and away the largest purchaser of this "editorial" advertising has long been the Mexican government. It has been widely reported that a banner headline and dominant front page story in *Excelsior*, Mexico City's largest daily, can be bought for about $200,000 U.S.

MAKING IT WORK

Obtaining professional advertising assistance is as simple in Mexico as in the United States. The risk factor will be relatively higher, not because of a lack of available professional expertise, but because of the same factors that often impinge upon the success of products introduced in the U.S. These can be summed up in one phrase: ignoring fundamentals. On your home turf, in markets you know both demographically and geographically, if an error is committed, you can effect damage control and make course changes quickly to maximize effectiveness.

In Mexico, it will be more difficult for you to tick off your fundamentals checklist preceding a media buy for a variety of reasons, including the lack of published research by product category. This affects pricing and competitive positioning strategy and can be compounded by lack of feedback from the distribution system. You may think the pipeline is full, but when your campaign breaks, the merchandise may still be in the warehouse, not on store shelves.

Media rates and the data upon which they are based (i.e., readership, viewing or listening audience) are not always available in a form that you can understand. This does not imply that rate setting is unfair; it merely points out that if you do not understand the media habits of the demographic sector you are trying to reach or how to determine the media you should employ to reach them, do exactly what you would do in the United States if you were opening a new territory—hire a professional who does know.

Media resources are abundant in Mexico, with the usual concentration of newspapers, radio and television stations, and outdoor billboards in the most populous areas. There are also a number of magazines and publications other than newspapers that target specific audiences.

Most of the services offered in the United States are available through Mexican media as well. The "800" number is used for direct response for everything from pain relief medication to sporting goods, just as in the United States.

Here is a brief look at some of the important media.

NEWSPAPERS

The leading daily papers in Mexico City are *Reforma*, *Excelsior*, *El Universal*, the *News* (in English), *El Heraldo*, *El Financiero* (business news, nationwide), and *El Economista* (business news, nationwide). There are a slew of other "popular" papers, some specializing in sports, others in scandal and graphic, grisly police reporting, and others just catering to a more common level of the public.

Some of these publish multiple editions. With the papers and all the editions, well over nine million newspapers are reportedly sold daily in Mexico City. Beware of circulation numbers, as they are not audited. At this time, only *El Norte* in Monterrey and *Reforma* and *El Universal* in Mexico City provide audited circulation figures.

Monterrey's leading papers are *El Norte* (in our opinion, far and away the best newspaper in Mexico) and *El Diario*. *El*

Norte so dominates this market that other local papers fade into relative insignificance by comparison. *El Financiero* and *El Economista* also have good penetration among the business community and have editorial offices in Monterrey.

Guadalajara's leading papers are *El Informador, Ocho Columnas,* and *Siglo XXI* (a well-received new paper). Again, as in Monterrey, *El Financiero* and *El Economista* are effective among the business community.

RADIO

Some nine hundred radio stations, AM and FM, are distributed throughout the nation, with special concentrations in major cities and populous states. There are estimated to be over eighteen million sets in use. As in the U.S., programming is designed to appeal to specific audiences at different times of the day.

The biggest network nationwide is StereoRey. Its news program is particularly effective because so many listen as they drive the interminable distances between points in Mexico City. Airtime in Mexico City is extremely expensive, though. In Monterrey and Guadalajara, the same programs on StereoRey are a fraction of the cost and equally effective in reaching their demographic target.

TELEVISION

Television reaches approximately twelve million households in Mexico. Again, the concentration is in the largest markets. The market has long been controlled by two entities, the government-owned channels and Televisa, owned by Emilio Azcarraga, the wealthiest man in Mexico. The 1993 *Forbes* list of the wealthiest people in the world estimated his wealth at over $5 billion U.S.

This monopoly has kept TV advertising rates in the stratosphere. However, the government sold its two channels to TV Azteca, which is now competing aggressively with Televisa. Don't be shy in negotiating rates with either network. Discount advertising packages can be negotiated.

Cable and satellite TV have made enormous inroads into the viewing habits of affluent Mexicans. There are probably more satellite antennae per capita in Monterrey than anywhere else in North America. CNN and HBO are now viewing staples throughout the country. HBO has begun a new Spanish-language service called HBOlé.

BILLBOARDS

Large markets such as Monterrey, Mexico City, and Guadalajara have the lion's share of outdoor showings. The key elements to be alert to here are *sizes* (because they use metric measurement) and the language used in the contracts describing the boards. Whether they require paper, paint, or vinyl varies as much in Mexico as in the U.S. On a creative note, ad agency art directors will be delighted with the variety of shapes and sizes that are available, as well as the lighting and special effects that may be added.

Most billboard companies will insist at the start that they can only work with a six-month minimum contract. As you point out the number of empty boards available and offer to pay on time, this, like everything else, is negotiable. As in the U.S., prices can vary *widely*. We've been quoted prices varying over 200 percent by competing companies for equivalent boards in the same market, in roughly the same locations.

The key phrase here is *caveat emptor*, as with the purchase of precious stones: "If you don't know diamonds, know your jeweler." There are excellent media facilitators or expediters available in Mexico, and a few well-schooled professionals in the U.S. who can access them for you and solve the problems before they arise. Use them.

A brief hint on buying billboards in Mexico City: unless you're going to put up a *lot* of them, don't bother. You will notice as you drive around the city how saturated the roadways are with boards. As big as the city is, and with so many boards competing for drivers' attention, you really need to cover some ground. Of course there are exceptions to this rule—if you put up a spectacular, eye-grabbing board in a well-researched *key* location, you can do very well indeed.

MAGAZINES

Without going into great detail, there are several excellent magazines published in Mexico. You will find that both the content and the printing are superb.

The top business magazine is *Expansión*. This is a serious business journal, read by most of the country's top execs. *Entrepreneur* has recently begun a Mexican edition, which is taking off well. *Proceso* is a widely read and quoted politically oriented weekly news magazine.

Depending on your target market, your ad agency can undoubtedly recommend many others. There are targeted publications for industry, as well as all segments of the public audience.

CHAPTER 11

THE ART OF GETTING PAID

Con dinero baila el perro.

[The dog dances for money.]

Well, now you know about the culture, the language, shipping, etc.—on to the really important stuff . . . How do you get paid?

First rule of thumb: specify payment in U.S. dollars. Not only is it nearly impossible to exchange pesos in the U.S., but you pay a premium to the bank for changing them. Not even God can help if you get a regular check (not a cashier's check) in pesos. Even along the border where they're used to working with Mexico, banks are stymied by peso checks.

We have been the unwilling recipients of peso checks on a number of occasions, and they have taken anywhere from a minimum of four weeks to more than six months to exchange, or even just to get a reply from the Mexican bank as to the availability of funds. This is a fool's game where everybody plays the float against you, holding onto your money as long as possible and charging outrageous transaction fees in the process. A peso check equal to about one thousand U.S. dollars can run up bank and wire charges of one hundred fifty dollars or more.

There are several methods of payment commonly employed in trade with Mexico:

1. Full payment in advance.

2. COD at the border. This can be done through:
    a. cash payment to your customs broker/freight forwarder as the shipment changes hands.
    b. a letter of credit paying directly into your bank upon presentation of delivery documents.

3. A letter of credit—terms as negotiated by both parties.

4. 50 percent deposit, with 50 percent on delivery at the border. This is recommended in any situation where you have to special order items to fill the customer's order. It also assures you of both the customer's commitment and your shipping costs to the border should the order be canceled. The 50 percent balance can be collected as described in 2 above.

5. Extending some form of credit—both the least common and least recommended course of action. Only to be offered after long-term experience with the client.

This warning against extending credit is not occasioned by Mexico having a particularly bad credit history; it's just that, once your merchandise leaves the U.S., legal remedies become infinitely more complicated should problems arise. How would you enforce payment if your customer reneges? How would you address claims for damages in transit when you don't have an agent on site? Suppose there's a customs or tax demand once the product is over the border and out of your control? These are but a few of the potential problems that could arise.

In most cases, credit won't be an issue. Mexican business works much more on a cash basis than U.S. business does. Extended payment terms are not yet as common as in the U.S. Should credit become a factor in your negotiating, there is a potential solution that merits looking into.

Through the Ex-Im Bank you can purchase foreign credit insurance. The program is called the Foreign Credit Insurance Administration (FCIA) and works in conjunction with your bank, insuring the value of your goods for export, along with a margin of profit, should any of the above situations arise.

Our advice, though, is keep it simple, unless credit becomes a deal-maker issue. Get paid in full on the U.S. side of the border under one of the methods outlined above. You'll sleep a lot better at night knowing where your merchandise is and how you're going to get paid.

If you're utilizing letters of credit, a few simple hints can keep you out of serious trouble. Talk to your banker first. If he or she doesn't have experience with international letters of credit, shop around until you find someone who does. What you want is a confirmed, irrevocable letter of credit. "Irrevocable" means that the buyer can't unilaterally cancel the letter from the other end, and "confirmed" means that your bank has confirmed the method by which it will receive the funds and is therein guaranteeing the payment to you.

When writing the terms of the letter of credit, give yourself as much leeway as possible on delivery or shipment dates. This is the area where most problems arise with LCs. And, while other problems can often be more easily remedied, a later-than-promised shipment requires that your customer in Mexico authorize a bank to amend the terms of the LC. This in itself is a fairly simple action, but it leaves you wide open to having your client take a hard-line approach and want to renegotiate the deal—asking for a discount or canceling the order because you're late. Once you've failed to meet any of the terms written into the LC, it's open season for renegotiations, which brings us to the next point.

Take care with *all* of the terms in the LC—if you want your money quickly, specify a "sight" letter of credit. This will pay you within days of the time the banker verifies that the paperwork is in order. LCs can be written with any payment terms you and your customer agree to. If you're not in any hurry, or aren't paying attention, you could have a letter that pays you six months or more after the banker signs off on it.

Normally, you pay the fees at your end, and your customer pays the fees at his or her end. If one of you is a better negotiator, then all fees will be paid by the other.

In all cases, caution is the watchword. Be conservative in your promises and cautious in your wording. Deal with a banker you know and trust, who is experienced in international trade and finance.

CHAPTER 12

ECONOMICS AND THE BANKING SYSTEM

Put not your trust in money,
but put your money in trust.

OLIVER WENDELL HOLMES, SR.

ECONOMIC POLICY

In 1985 Mexico began formulating the new economic policy that has resulted in the near miraculous opening of its markets and expansion of its economy. Most analysts agree that Mexico's primary objective for pursuing trade liberalization was to improve the competitiveness of its domestic industry and, since late 1987, to fight inflation.

Mexico has been enormously successful in winning the inflation battle. The 1992 inflation rate was 11.9 percent, compared with 160 percent when Salinas took office in 1988.

The Salinas administration pursued policies aimed at opening the economy as rapidly as possible. His policies encouraged foreign investment, promoted non-oil exports, and reformed import policies. By reducing the number of state-owned companies he successfully lowered government outlays as a proportion of GDP.

THE BANKING SYSTEM

On September 1, 1982, outgoing President José López Portillo shocked Mexico's financial community by announcing that the Mexican government had taken over all the privately owned banks in the country, except the branches of Citibank, N.A., and the representative offices of foreign banks.

This was the final nail in the coffin for investor confidence and any semblance of economic stability in Mexico. Capital, which had been leaving Mexico at an alarming rate following the steep devaluations of that and the previous year, now hemorrhaged out of every financial artery. Cash flew over the border into U.S. and offshore banks in tens of billions of dollars.

It is widely acknowledged now that this nationalization of the banks was absolutely the worst economic move that could have been made at a very sensitive time of crisis. At the beginning of 1981, the peso was being traded at 23+ to the dollar. By the end of 1982, when President López Portillo grabbed the banks, it was trading at over 300:1.

Over the course of the next six years, confidence in the economic system was nonexistent. Over $90 billion is estimated to have been taken out of the country in that period. The exchange rate plunged through 1,000:1, then 2,000:1, and stabilized at just over 3,000:1.

With government management of all banks, competition disappeared along with credibility. Service levels were dismally poor. Waste and inefficiency ran rampant. Needless to say, operating profits were poor as well.

Compensation was paid to the former private shareholders of the banks through Bank Indemnization bonds of the federal government which matured in 1992; these bonds had quarterly interest payments at the average rates for three and six months' deposits at the banks.

Mexico's banks are divided into two groups, development banks and commercial banks. The development banks include those previously established by the government for special purposes, such as financing farm operations, export trade, and housing developments. Nacional Financiera, S.A., operates as the principal government bank for promoting the development of industry. Most loans in foreign currency to the Mexican government or its agencies are channeled through this bank.

The commercial banks receive the great majority of checking and savings deposits and provide most of the short-term credit. The four largest banks (Banamex, Bancomer, Comermex, and Serfin) operate through a total of over 2,000 branches throughout the country. The commercial banks also provide longer-term loans for capital goods and real estate mortgage loans, as well as for financing inventories and receivables. Nevertheless, loans are not made for periods of more than seven to ten years.

Reversal of Fortunes

From the time we began work on this manuscript to the present, Mexico's banking system has made a complete turnaround from government bureaucracy back to private business. The process began in 1982 when then-president José López Portillo, in the final act of his presidency, nationalized the country's entire banking system. When his own disastrous economic policies resulted in an unprecedented flight of capital from the country, López Portillo decided the banks were at fault, and the solution was for the government to seize the banks.

Already shaken by the precipitous fall of the peso, and rocked by spiraling inflation, those investors who had not yet removed their money from the country viewed the bank seizures as the final act of insanity in a series of suicidal economic errors. López Portillo is widely suspected of having looted billions of dollars from the country's treasury in his six-year reign. To this day he is greeted by barking and howls from the Mexican public, remembering a 1982 speech in which he promised to defend Mexico's economy "like a dog."

After watching the economy suffer nearly a decade of stultifying bureaucratic mismanagement, and public mistrust of government-controlled banking, the Salinas administration began the process of reprivatization in 1991. Bidding was frenzied among private investment groups wishing to cash in on Mexico's exciting economic future.

First to go was Banco Mercantil, which sold to the Probursa Group for 2.66 times its book value. Using some of the smaller banks to gauge the market's strength, the government then put Mexico's two flagship financial institutions on the block in August and October 1991. Banamex, Mexico's largest bank, brought a winning bid of $3.08 billion U.S. This was more than two and a half times its book value.

When Mexico's number two bank, Bancomer, was auctioned off two months later, the VAMSA group of Monterrey, headed by Grupo VISA magnate Eugenio Garza Lagüera, won with a bid of $2.48 billion U.S—nearly three times its book value.

With all the banks having been sold off, investors paid an average of three times the book value or 14.75 times earnings. Mexico's treasury reaped an incredible windfall of nearly $12 billion U.S. This was used to retire a substantial amount of the government's internal debt.

Now that banking is back in private hands, competition among the banks is heating up. Marked improvements in services and products are being experienced throughout the system. Even more changes are anticipated with the implementation of the North American Free Trade Agreement.

Financial services have been addressed in the agreement, and a progressive opening of this market to foreign institutions is expected. Having helped finance the rebuilding of Mexico after its revolution, Citibank has long enjoyed privileged status as the only foreign financial institution allowed to maintain full-service banking operations there. It appears that it will not enjoy this unique position much longer.

To facilitate trade both domestically and internationally, new denominations of currency were issued on January 1, 1993, eliminating three 0s. Thus the 10,000 peso bill became the N$10 bill, etc. (N$ is the official symbol for "new pesos.") The design and form of the paper currency remained the same as before, with only the 0s missing. Much to every-one's relief, smaller and lighter coins were also minted. The value of the currency remained as before, but calculating prices and exchange rates is much simpler. The peso went from 3,000:1 to about 3 to the dollar. By June 1996 the peso had fallen back to 7.5 to the dollar.

International Banking

Foreign banks are showing a renewed interest in the market. Many U.S. banks are once again seeking to finance invest-ments in Mexico. In 1991 Morgan Guarantee provided $1.5 billion U.S. in bridge loans to the VAMSA group out of Mon-terrey which purchased Bancomer.

Apart from the financing of specific projects, the Mexi-can banking law currently allows three basic types of for-eign bank presence in the country: representation, agency, or branch. The principal functions of foreign bank offices in Mexico can be summed up as follows:

1. Representations: This means a direct presence in a given market to promote business generated or consoli-dated in that market, as well as negotiating credit lines with other banks or financial institutions, particularly to support foreign trade activities. Staff of the represen-tative office are prohibited from directly soliciting de-positors' business.

2. Agencies: These have the same basic functions as do representative offices, plus being able to approve hard-currency credits for both national and foreign clients; provide lines of credit; and provide international trea-sury services and the attraction of new funds for corpo-rate deposit accounts with some limitations, such as di-rect deposits by residents of the country where the agency is established.

3. Branches: These offices operate pretty much as do agencies, but they can attract deposits without any

limitations and can also provide trust services. At the moment, only Citibank enjoys this status.

Current Bank Investment Products

Bank investments are currently limited to savings deposits, time deposits, private bank acceptances, and subordinated bank debentures.

These savings vehicles, like their U.S. counterparts, offer interest rates that vary according to the size of the deposit and the length of the term. At the time of writing this book, the interest rates offered on peso investments were *very* attractive—if you're willing to run the risk of devaluation, the rewards can be significant.

Other Investment Options

The Mexican Stock Exchange offers three vehicles for foreign investors to acquire securities issued by Mexican corporations:

1. Full Subscription Shares: similar to U.S. stocks; holders of these shares have the same voting rights as Mexican investors. The National Foreign Investment Commission does, however, regulate the maximum percentage of shares that can be held by foreign investors. More than half of the principal companies listed on the Mexican Stock Exchange allow foreign stock ownership, and many of these permit foreign investors to hold a majority position.

2. American Depository Receipts or ADRs: These are Mexican companies whose shares are listed outside the country through ADRs. The shares are negotiable receipts backing securities of the issuing company. These securities are held in trust by a banking institution.

3. Foreign Investment Trust Fund: This is an option resulting from a provision of the New Regulations for

Foreign Investment. Under these new regulations foreign investors can acquire shares exclusively reserved for Mexican citizens represented by ordinary participation certificates. These certificates confer property rights only, not voting rights.

International arbitrage is also currently authorized between Mexican brokerage firms and foreign brokers. This provides the investor with the option to take advantage of the price differential between common shares of the same stock issues on different markets.

MEXICO'S CHANGING FINANCIAL LANDSCAPE

On July 18, 1990, the Mexican government approved the law to regulate financial groups. Expectations are that this major step in Mexico's financial reform will spur renewed growth in savings that will in turn provide greater investment capital. This will be achieved by balancing the Mexican financial system through the consolidation of various financial services into cohesive groups.

Under the new regulations financial groups can be structured through a holding company that includes at least three of the following:

Bank
Bonding Company
Brokerage Firm
Financial Factoring Company
Financial Leasing Firm
Foreign Exchange Firm
General Deposit Warehouse
Insurance Company
Mutual Fund Operator

The regulations are designed to prevent the concentration of credits within a single company, and it is contemplated that industries or trading companies will form financial groups. The holding company could not assume liabilities and could only be responsible for administering the financial groups' shares. The business activities of groups' operating entities would be kept separate, and separate sets of books would be maintained.

The concept of universal banking is a worldwide trend, and Mexico is rapidly gearing up for the sweeping changes that began in the eighties and will continue through the nineties. Offering a broad array of services under one roof will benefit the consumer through convenience and more competitive margins.

These very positive moves are substantially strengthening Mexico's financial underpinning and promise real stability in the country's economic future (see Table 1 for a chart chronicling the reprivatization of Mexico's banks).

TABLE 1. REPRIVATIZATION OF MEXICO'S BANKING SYSTEM

BANK	DATE SOLD	BUYER	SALE PRICE (thousands of dollars)	MULTIPLE OF BOOK VALUE
MERCANTIL	June 7, 1991	Probursa	$ 194,031	2.66
BANPAIS	June 14, 1991	Mexival	173,012	3.02
CREMI	June 21, 1991	R. Gómez	237,552	3.40
CONFIA	Aug. 2, 1991	Abaco	283,257	3.73
BANORIENTE	Aug. 9, 1991	G. Margen	70,864	4.00
BANCRECER	Aug. 16, 1991	R. Alcántara	134,644	2.53
BANAMEX	Aug. 23, 1991	Accival	3,081,301	2.62
BANCOMER	Oct. 25, 1991	VAMSA	2,476,048	2.99
B.C.H.	Nov. 8, 1991	C. Cabal	278,844	2.67
SERFIN	Jan. 24, 1992	Operadora de Bolsa	897,695	2.69
COMERMEX	Feb. 7, 1992	Inverlat	859,052	2.73
SOMEX	Feb. 21, 1992	Inverméxico	595,722	3.31
ATLANTICO	Mar. 27, 1992	G.B.M.	466,400	5.30
PROMEX	Apr. 3, 1992	Valores Finamex	341,103	4.23
BANORO	Apr. 10, 1992	Estrategia Bursatil	361,241	3.95
BANORTE	June 14, 1992	Roberto González	563,739	4.25
INTERNACIONAL	June 28, 1992	Prime	472,037	2.95

CHAPTER 13

THE MEXICAN POLITICAL SYSTEM

> In politics, all friends are false and
> all enemies are real.
> GUSTAVO DÍAZ ORDAZ
>
> *Un político pobre es un pobre político.*
> [A politician who's poor is a poor politician.]
> ATTRIBUTED TO CARLOS HANK GONZÁLEZ

Government plays a dominant role in nearly all aspects of daily life in Mexico, and this especially applies to business. Although it has divested itself of most of the nationalized companies it once owned, the government still regulates most business activities to one degree or another.

No matter what your field of endeavor, you will eventually find yourself in line at some government office waiting interminably for some form or document to be drawn up or approved. Your eyes will glaze over as the fourteenth secretary of the twelfth *licenciado* tells you to take a seat and fill out the next form.

The key to good business in Mexico is understanding the system and having good contacts who can help you expedite the glacial movement of paper through the system. You will also be well served by knowing a bit about the structure of that government.

Mexico is a federal republic constituted by thirty-one states and the Federal District (D.F.), better known as Mexico City. The political constitution of the United Mexican States is the fundamental law upon which the overall organization of the country is based. The Mexican constitution is one of the most advanced constitutions in the world regarding social guarantees. The supreme power of the federation is divided into three branches: the executive, judicial, and legislative powers.

The supreme executive power is vested in a single individual, the president of the United Mexican States. The judicial power is vested in the Supreme Court of Justice, circuit courts, collegiate courts for habeas corpus, and unitary courts for appeals, as well as district courts. Finally, the legislative power is deposited in a General Congress, which is divided into two chambers, a Chamber of Deputies and a Senate.

Deputies, who are elected by proportional districts, serve a three-year term and may not be reelected. There are 500 deputies serving in the congress, as well as 64 senators.

The senators represent their states, and there are two for every state and the Federal District. They serve a six-year term and may not be reelected.

The government of the Federal District corresponds to the president of the Republic, who has the power to delegate or exercise this function through another person appointed by him who is known as regent of the Department of the Federal District. For better control of services and administrative activities, the Federal District is divided into sixteen political delegations which act in an autonomous manner and have an independent budget, but which are coordinated by the regent of the Department of the Federal District.

Each state has roughly the same political structure as the federal government, with a powerful chief executive, who answers to the president in Mexico City.

POWERS OF THE PRESIDENT

Since the revolution, Mexican presidents have been allowed to serve only one six-year term in office, during which they enjoy near absolute power to rule. Indeed, few of the world's leaders are granted such complete license in their country's affairs as the Mexican president. In exchange for these six years of absolute power, the president is expected to totally disappear from the political scene, never to return again. This precedent was set by Lázaro Cárdenas in April 1936, when he escorted outgoing president Plutarco Elías Calles to a waiting plane, for a gentle exile in Los Angeles. Calles had shown too great an enthusiasm for the office, and a reluctance to depart the stage.

The president is given specific powers under the constitution as well as those conferred by law:

- To declare a state of siege.

- To intervene in the states (this includes appointing replacement governors for those appointed to cabinet offices, incapacitated by illness, or forcibly removed from office—by July 1992, Salinas had appointed twelve governors out of a total of thirty-two).

- To appoint his cabinet, the attorney general, and the governor of the Federal District and to remove members (without consulting Congress).

- To promulgate laws.

- To veto legislation.

- To issue basic rules that flesh out statutes (most legislation in Mexico is in the form of these basic rules).

- To appoint (with the approval of the Senate) diplomatic officials, higher officers of the army, and ministers of the cabinet.

- To direct the armed forces for internal and external security.

- To sponsor legislation (legislation sponsored by the executive takes precedence in Congress).

- To grant pardons.

The following presidential powers are conferred by law:

- To name the directors and assistant directors of the semiautonomous agencies of the federal government.

- To intervene in industrial and commercial activities.

- To control monetary policy.

- To control and regulate foreign investment.

- To intervene in the education system to make plans for teacher training.

- To compile and update primary school texts.

- To grant and revoke concessions for radio and television channels.

- To control the supply of newsprint to the national press (the newsprint-producing and -importing company is state owned).

In addition, the president also has broad powers in foreign policy and controls the executive branch and the parastatal industries.

POLITICAL PARTIES

Among Mexico's political parties are:

PRI	Institutional Revolutionary Party
PAN	National Action Party
PRD	Revolutionary Democratic Party
PARM	Authentic Party of the Mexican Revolution
PCM	Mexican Communist Party
PDM	Mexican Democratic Party
PMS	Mexican Socialist Party
PMT	Mexican Workers' Party
PPS	Popular Socialist Party
PRT	Revolutionary Workers' Party

PSD   Socialist Democratic Party
PST   Socialist Workers' Party
PSUM   Unified Socialist Party of Mexico

With such a variety of parties, Mexican society has several options, ideologies, and political systems to choose from during elections. Among this plethora of parties, three stand out. The PRI is *the* ruling party and has been since the revolution sparked its formation in the 1920s. PAN is the conservative competition, now beginning to make some inroads into the PRI's total domination of the national political scene. And drawing up the vocal rear is the PRD, the isolationist, xenophobic party led by Cuauhtémoc Cárdenas, son of former president Lázaro Cárdenas.

The PRD and many observers claim that their candidate, Cárdenas, actually won the 1988 presidential campaign. In fact, their claim may not be terribly farfetched, in view of the universal disgust of the entire population with the condition of the economy and the management of the government. Whether by luck or manipulation, though, the country's best interests were well served by the results, and today the PRD has lost its appeal to the vast majority of voters.

ELECTIONS

Mexico has no popular primary elections. The internal nominating process of the various parties fulfills that role. Those that have been selected as candidates then run in an election where they compete for the popular vote.

Presidential elections have, for the last seventy-five years, been a platform for the PRI to showcase its chosen presidential successor. They serve the following purposes:

• Conveying the image of Mexico as a democracy

• Maintaining continuity with the origins of the revolution

• Sounding public opinion in various areas

- Providing an opportunity for citizens to become involved in the political process

- Enabling each president to get to know the country and the country to get to know the president

This uncontested hold on national office was first seriously challenged in 1988, when Cuauhtémoc Cárdenas ran on the PRD's party ticket and, some aver, actually won the popular vote against declared winner Carlos Salinas de Gortari. The president serves a six-year term and may not be reelected; there is no vice-president. The presidential nominee of the PRI is selected by the president, which means, in effect, because of the predominance of the PRI, that the president selects a successor.

The president is elected by popular vote.

State elections are held every six years for the election of the governor, and every three years for local representatives. These elections are subject to the provisions of the local constitution of each state.

Key Governmental Agencies

Depending upon your business interests or requirements, you will probably require assistance from one or more of the following key government agencies in the course of doing business:

- Presidency

  Presidencia de la República
  Phone: (Residence—
  Los Pinos) 515-7807;
  515-5726
  (Presidential Palace)
  542-8070

- Secretariat of Commerce and Industrial Promotion

  Secretaría de Comercio y Fomento Industrial (SECOFI)

- Secretariat of Foreign Relations — Secretaría de Relaciones Exteriores (SRE)

- Secretariat of the Treasury and Public Credit — Secretaría de Hacienda y Crédito Público (SHCP)

- Secretariat of Tourism — Secretaría de Turismo (SECTUR)

- Secretariat of Agriculture and Water Resources — Secretaría de Agricultura y Recursos Hidráulicos (SARH)

- Secretariat of Communications and Transportation — Secretaría de Comunicaciones y Transportes (SCT)

- Secretariat of Health — Secretaría de Salud (SSA)

- Justice Department — Procuraduría General de la República (PGR)

- Secretariat of Government — Secretaría de Gobernación (SG) (a unique, extremely powerful agency that controls internal governing of the country, elections, etc.)

- Secretariat of Social Development — Secretaría de Desarrollo Social (SEDESOL) (administers federal social programs)

- Secretariat of Fishing and the Environment — Secretaría de Pesca y Medio Ambiente

- Secretariat of National Defense — Secretaría de la Defensa Nacional

- Secretariat of Public Education — Secretaría de Educación Pública

- Secretariat of Labor and Social Welfare
- Secretariat of Energy
- Secretariat of Agrarian Reform
- Comptroller General of the Federation
- Secretariat of the Navy
- City Government of Mexico City

Secretaría de Trabajo y Previsión Social

Secretaría de Energía

Secretaría de Reforma Agraria

Secretaría de la Contraloría General de la Federación

Secretaría de la Marina

Departamento del Distrito Federal (DDF) (Mexico City's mayor, called the *regente*, is one of the top three or four political powers in the country)

CHAPTER 14

TRAVELING FOR BUSINESS IN MEXICO

Poco a poco se va lejos.

[Little by little one goes a long way.]

DOCUMENTATION

Requirements are simple but rigid: proof of U.S. citizenship and a tourist visa. Proof of citizenship can be a passport, birth certificate, or voter registration (the latter two must be accompanied by a photo ID, preferably a driver's license). The tourist visa can be obtained from the Mexican consulate in your area, a travel agent or airline, or at the border.

If you are actually going to operate a business in Mexico or work for an extended period you must have a U.S. passport and a Mexican work permit. These are not difficult to acquire; however, you should allow at least two weeks to receive your passport and several weeks for the processing of a work visa. The visa is obtained from the Mexican embassy or your nearest Mexican consulate.

For normal business travel involving stays of up to thirty days, or in-and-out business travel, a short-term business visa is available, called an FMN. It is good for thirty days and allows multiple entries into the country during that period. The FMN is easily obtained from a Mexican consulate or, in many cases, from the airline flying to Mexico or at immigration upon arrival in Mexico. To obtain an FMN from a consulate you will need your passport and a letter on company letterhead stating you will be in Mexico for business purposes. The consulate can issue the visa on the spot, much like the standard tourist card.

DRIVING IN MEXICO?!

We open this with an editorial opinion: If it is not absolutely necessary for you to drive in Mexico, *don't.*

Roger tells of his first day of orientation at college in Mexico, where the first pointer was: If you're in an accident and the car still runs, leave the scene immediately. If the car won't run, but you can, leave the car and take off! You can straighten out the details later from a safe distance.

Remember that Mexico observes the Napoleonic Code, which presumes guilt in any infraction. All parties are usually detained for investigation, and the involved vehicles are impounded until the claims are settled. You could be jailed for weeks or months pending settlement, which will never come out in your favor.

Mexican insurance may help in the major cities, but in small towns and out of the way villages, your fate is in the hands of the local authority, who may turn out to be the cousin of the fellow with whom you had the accident—not a situation you want to find yourself in.

Taxis and public transportation are cheap and liability free. Use them.

If you are traveling to Mexico for business we strongly recommend that you leave the driving to the pros. Taxicabs are plentiful in the major cities and hiring a car and driver can be an excellent investment as well. You won't have to worry about getting to meetings on time, parking, traffic tickets, insurance, or risk.

If you insist on driving in Mexico you will need the title to your car and *Mexican* insurance. The insurance must be obtained from a Mexican carrier and may be purchased in any U.S. border city.

Taking a car into Mexico requires a combination tourist

card or business visa and car permit. You will need your title and registration to receive the permit. If the car belongs to your company or any other owner you must have a notarized affidavit from the owner or lienholder authorizing you to take the car into Mexico.

The other requirements are a valid driver's license and current license plates.

A final note: Mexican law does not allow foreigners to sell their car in Mexico. Even if your car is disabled or demolished, be prepared to bring it back across the border by any means available (at your expense, of course).

CAR RENTALS

Again, not recommended. In the first place, renting a car in Mexico is very expensive. A Volkswagen can cost over eighty dollars per day, plus mileage, which could add another fifty dollars or more to the total. Add this to all of the abovementioned liabilities and you can easily see that hiring a taxi by the day not only makes life easier, but can save you a considerable amount of money.

CHANGING MONEY

Even if you're only going to be in Mexico briefly, you would do well to exchange some dollars for pesos. While dollars are widely accepted, you can't be sure of the rate of exchange you may get outside of the banks and exchange houses.

Banks are normally open from 9 A.M. until 1:30 P.M. on weekdays. There are also money exchange houses (*casas de cambio*). These exchanges are legal outlets, and you may want to compare their rates with those at the banks. They also offer the advantage of longer hours, and some are open seven days a week.

The exchange windows at the Mexico City airport are nearly always open and offer rates comparable to those in town. This is one of the easiest and most convenient places to exchange money upon arrival, so that you have taxi fare, bellhop tips, etc.

On January 1, 1993, new currency was issued, to reduce the confusion inherent in the large-denomination bills in circulation. The new bills are essentially the same as the old, less three decimal places. Thus, the old 10,000 peso bill has become the N$10. Wherever prices are written, the new symbol is N$, for "new pesos."

When you change your money, ask for a mix that includes a substantial mix of N$2, 5, and 10 coins and N$10 and 20 denomination bills for taxis, tips, and meals. Have N$20 and 50 bills for larger purchases. Keep plenty of the smaller bills handy, as taxis and small shopkeepers often do not have change for larger denominations.

Personal checks are very difficult to cash. Plan on paying with cash or a credit card for everything.

WHERE TO STAY

Principal Business Hotels

First impressions count in Mexico. If you're going to be receiving calls or visitors at your hotel, then you want to stay in one of the recognized leading properties.

This is by no means a comprehensive tourist guide— you will have no trouble finding many wonderful books on the varied attractions for the holiday traveler. This listing is specifically aimed at the business traveler. We have included here our favorite business-class hotels in Mexico City, Guadalajara, and Monterrey. You'll want to contact your travel agent for reservations and *confirmations*, but rest assured that if you choose one of these hotels you can't go far wrong on a business trip.

Be aware that when checking into hotels in Mexico, you are asked to *sign* a blank credit card voucher. This is standard practice and should not alarm you.

Note: When figuring your travel costs, add 10 percent value added tax (IVA) onto almost everything, restaurant and hotel bills included. Also, be aware that long distance phone calls in Mexico are very expensive, particularly from hotels which add a service charge—several times what you are used to paying from the U.S.—so if you need to call home, be brief (a typical call back to the office can easily cost $30–$40!). You can save lots of money by calling collect, or plan ahead to have your office and/or loved ones call you at specific times. Direct dial rates from the U.S. are not bad.

An exhibitor in one of our trade shows called the travel agent in an absolute panic after receiving her hotel bill. She hadn't paid attention to the warning about phone bills on the travel information we had given out before the show. She and her associate ran up over three thousand dollars in phone calls over five days! Remember, keep it short and sweet!

Mexico City   (There are so many hotels here in the largest city in the world that this is in no way a complete guide. These are the most-frequented and well-known business hotels in the capital.)

Four Seasons—The city's most elegant new hotel. Tastefully built in colonial style around a beautiful courtyard, this is *the* place to be (if you can afford it!).
Address: Paseo de la Reforma 500
Telephone: 286-6020

Maria Isabel Sheraton—Next door to the American embassy, near the Zona Rosa, this is the top gringo hotel in the city. Reliable, quality accommodations, central location.
Address: Paseo de la Reforma 325
Telephone: 207-3933

Nikko Hotel—A stylish, relatively new entrant in the capital hotel sweepstakes, direct competitor to the Camino Real for the top ranking. Owned by Japan Air Lines, near Chapultepec Park, on the edge of fashionable Polanco, walking distance to the Anthropology Museum.

Address: Campos Elíseos No. 204
Telephone: 203-4020
   Presidente Inter-Continental—First-class property next door to the Nikko. This has been one of the city's top hotels for years.
Address: Campos Elíseos 218
Telephone: 327-7788
   Camino Real—Forever the top hotel in Mexico City, but new blood in the market might make the Camino look a little dog-eared by comparison, though you wouldn't know it by the sky-high prices.
Address: Mariano Escobedo 700
Telephone: 203-2121
   Westin Galería Plaza—A reliable Zona Rosa business location, the Galería Plaza is a respectable address that won't break the bank.
Address: Hamburgo 195
Telephone: 211-0014
   Nuevo Hotel Marquis Reforma—Brand new, super polished, and glitzy. If the prices don't give you nosebleed, this is the place. On Reforma, halfway between the U.S. Embassy and Chapultepec Park.
Address: Paseo de la Reforma 465
Telephone: 211-3140
   Holiday Inn Crowne Plaza—Another top-quality property, complete with restaurants and bars galore. The nightclub features some of the country's top names in show business.
Address: Paseo de la Reforma 80
Telephone: 705-1515
   Hotel María Cristina—A small, discreet insider's spot, one block off Reforma, near the U.S. Embassy, possessing the most peaceful garden for breakfast or drinks. Nothing fancy or pretentious, but room rates too low to believe. We've stayed here whenever possible for the last twenty years. See if one of the master suites is available. (Shhh . . . our secret!)

Address: Lerma No. 31
Telephone: 566-9688
  Radisson—In Pedregal, on the far south side of the city. If your business is in this part of town, this is the place to stay.
Address: Cúspide No. 53
Telephone: 606-9809
  Without going into great detail, some others are worth mentioning:
  Along Reforma: the *Emporio* and the *Imperial.*
  In the Zona Rosa: the *Krystal*, the *Century*, and the *Calinda Geneve.*
  Downtown: the *Majestic* and the *Howard Johnson Grand Hotel*, both right on the Zócalo, or main plaza.
  There are many, many other good hotels in town, among them some real "finds." But Mexico City is so big that no business traveler will ever discover them all. These we've listed are the ones we know well, by experience and by reputation. If you discover a good new one, please let us know.

Guadalajara   Mexico's second largest city offers some of the most delightful places to stay for either business or pleasure. With the area's incredible golf courses, pleasant weather, and great shopping, you'll find yourself looking for reasons to return often. It's also just thirty minutes by air from Puerto Vallarta, a nice place to wind down after a few days of business or a trade show at Expo Guadalajara.
  Quinta Real—The flagship of a new chain of hotels that have set the standard of quality for the competition. A beautiful hotel.
Address: Avenida México 2727
Telephone: 615-0000
  Camino Real—Roger's Guadalajara favorite: an elegant address, rambling, lush and green, peaceful, built around impeccably groomed lawns and gardens, with five pools. Directly across from the Chamber of Commerce.

Address: Av. Vallarta 5005
Telephone: 647-8000

Holiday Inn—Much more than you might expect from the name, this is a lovely spot, like the Camino Real, built around lawns and tropical foliage.
Address: Av. López Mateos Sur 2500
Telephone: 634-1034

Hyatt Regency—Across the street from the Plaza del Sol shopping center and close hotel to the exposition center, Expo Guadalajara. The attached shopping looks in on the Hyatt's beautiful grand ballroom.
Address: Av. López Mateos Sur y Moctezuma
Telephone: 622-7778

Fiesta Americana—Good central location, large modern facility, but lacking the character of the others. An efficient address for business, but you're not likely to long for a getaway weekend here.
Address: Aurelio Acéves 225
Telephone: 625-3434

Monterrey   Mexico's industrial capital is woefully under-supplied with hotel rooms, though it's home to some of the stateliest lobbies in the country. Best advice here is book early and get your confirmation in writing, particularly at the Crowne Plaza, where overbooking seems to be chronic.

Gran Hotel Ancira—A classic old-world gem, hands-down favorite of both authors. The marble and polished brass lobby sets the stage for the flawless service and attention to detail. Where the elite gather. Glenn maintained a semipermanent suite here for nearly seven years during the time he represented the Cuauhtémoc Breweries.
Address: Hidalgo y Escobedo
Telephone: 343-2060

Westin Ambassador—Another beauty, with a stained glass ceiling over the lobby dining room. On a par with the Ancira, elegant.

Address: Hidalgo y E. Carranza
Telephone: 342-2040

Holiday Inn Crowne Plaza—The most bustling of the major hotels. The show bar in the atrium lobby is the busiest in town, and the loudest—they had to install double doors in all the rooms to muffle the live music that plays seven nights a week.

Address: Avenida Constitución Ote. 300
Telephone: 319-6000

Fiesta Americana—Brand new: over the ridge in Garza García. A welcome addition to the perennially overbooked Monterrey hotel scene.

Address: José Vasconcelos 300 Ote.
Telephone: 363-3030

Two very welcome additions to the lodging scene in Monterrey are the Suites Hotel Antaris and the Holiday Inn Convention Center, both immediately adjacent to the fabulous Cintermex expo and convention center.

Valuables/Jewelry

Better hotels have safety deposit boxes (*cajas de seguridad*). Traveling in Mexico, like traveling anywhere, requires precaution, so use the facilities available.

BUSINESS TRAVEL

Where to Entertain Your Clients: The Power Lunch

The "power lunch" is an integral part of doing business in Mexico. Remember that lunch is the heaviest meal of the day for Mexicans. The executive lunch is usually taken from 2 P.M. to 4:30 P.M. You will find that most Mexicans like to start out with a *copa*, or cocktail, before eating.

If you want to impress your prospective clients, then don't take them to Sanborns (the Denny's of Mexico). Take them to a restaurant where Mexican executives eat. Remember to relax during lunch and socialize. Business will come in due time.

We recommend the following "power lunch" spots.

Mexico City   *San Angel Inn*—Continental cuisine
Address: Calle Palmas 50
Telephone: 548-6840
   La Hacienda de los Morales—Spanish and Mexican cuisine
Address: Vásquez de Mella 525
Telephone: 540-3225
   Bellinghausen—German cuisine
Address: Londres 95
Telephone: 511-9035
   Champs Elysee—French cuisine
Address: Amberes 1 (Corner of Reforma)
Telephone: 514-0450
   La Taberna de León
Address: 46 Altamirano, Plaza Loreto, San Angel
Telephone: 550-0989
   Winston Churchill—Continental cuisine
Address: Blvd. Avila Camacho No. 67
Telephone: 520-0585
   Maxim's—French cuisine (branch of Maxim's of Paris)
Address: Presidente Inter-Continental Hotel
Telephone: 254-0025
   Fouquet's—French cuisine (branch of Fouquet's of Paris)
Address: Camino Real Hotel
Telephone: 203-2121

It's hard to go wrong at any of the La Mansión steakhouses or Freedom restaurants.

Guadalajara   *Suehiro*—Japanese cuisine
Address: SJC—31-B No. 1701
Telephone: 625-1888
   Aquellos Tiempos—Continental cuisine
Address: Camino Real Hotel

Telephone: 614-1117
   La Destilería—Traditional Mexican
Address: Av. Mexico 2916
Telephone: 640-3440

Monterrey   *El Tío*—Mexican cuisine (cabrito)
Address: Hidalgo y México
Telephone: 346-0291
   El Granero—steaks
Address: Del Valle 333
Telephone: 378-0604
   Luisiana—Continental food
Address: Av. Hidalgo Ote. 530—Zona Rosa
Telephone: 343-1561
   La Guacamaya—Seafood
Address: Roble 515—Col. del Valle Campestre
Telephone: 378-7303
   Cinco Cero—Chinese cuisine
Address: Gómez Morín, Col. del Valle Campestre
Telephone: 378-6405

Tips (*Propinas*)

Standard tips are ten to fifteen percent in restaurants, three to six pesos per night for the chambermaid in a good hotel, the same per bag for porters, and ten percent of the fare for a taxi driver.

Social Drinking

Lunch normally begins with cocktails and winds up with a brandy afterward, before heading back to the office. This may take a little getting used to, but when in Rome . . .

If you're lunching in Mexico City, though, beware of the altitude. It's a mile and a half above sea level, and the thin air makes for a potent combination with alcohol.

Without a doubt, you will soon be introduced to tequila—be careful. Disguised in a luscious margarita or tequila sour, this alcoholic derivative of the maguey plant is insidious. As a Texas friend of ours stated, "Tequila makes you see double and feel single." He in fact recounts at least one near-religious experience after an evening that included a *mano a mano* bout with an experienced Mexican contender where shooters were the drink of choice.

Tequila is an excellent drink—just don't overdo it. Treat it with the same respect you have for a ninety proof gin martini. Limit your drinking and enjoy.

CHAPTER HIGHLIGHTS

We've included these chapter highlights to serve as a memory refresher and to assist you in locating information you may wish to review more thoroughly.

CHAPTER 1: MEXICO—THE MARKET

- Market size 87,000,000 and growing, at 2 percent per annum.

- Rapidly emerging middle class with the discretionary income to afford U.S.-made consumer products.

- Of the 26,000,000 middle- or upper-class consumers, most are located in the major cities.

CHAPTER 2: SEISMIC CHANGES

- Major step in opening Mexico's economy was President Miguel de la Madrid's application to join GATT (General Agreement on Trade and Tariffs) in 1985, prompted by his budget and planning minister, Carlos Salinas de Gortari.

- In 1988 President Salinas began an aggressive campaign to privatize government-owned businesses, including the telephone company, Telmex; the huge copper mines at Cananea; and the two national airlines.

- As a result of these and other equally dramatic measures, inflation, which had hovered at around 160 percent, declined to around 20 percent within a two-year period and the peso restabilized.

- President Salinas' dedication to the formulation of a Free Trade Agreement between the United States and Mexico bore fruit.

- Many Mexican business categories have been opened to foreign ownership without prior government approval.

CHAPTER 3: WHEN IN ROME

- Mexicans are extremely conscious of their history and revere tradition. Never forget that they are a proud people.

- Be patient in your attempts to establish business relationships. Remember Mexicans have a historical right to be skeptical of any foreigners' interest in their country or their business.

- Establish your reputation by meeting every commitment you make.

- Mexicans are shrewd negotiators, deliberate and cautious; it will pay for you to cool your natural aggression and use the time to explore their offerings as thoroughly as they will review yours.

- Word of your performance will spread rapidly on the Mexican business grapevine. Make certain that the reports are always positive.

- Keep your appointments, but do not criticize your

Mexican counterpart for being tardy or for keeping you waiting. It is bad form.

- Make allowances in your daily scheduling of successive meetings for the possible late start of earlier meetings. Don't look at your watch and don't hurry the meeting.

CHAPTER 4: MAKING CONTACT

- Try to establish initial contact with a key decision maker. Be patient, do your research, and know who you need to contact in that all-important first meeting.

- Networking is vital; if you don't know where to start, contract with a qualified consultant before you go to Mexico. In the United States, we commonly have someone "front us in"; it works the same way in Mexico.

- Research Mexican chamber of commerce membership rosters for your business category. Unlike U.S. chambers, each Mexican chamber is dedicated to a specific industry.

- Government contacts are important as well; cultivate those that affect your business at a state or federal level and pay your respects to the officials in the city or area you wish to do business in.

- Any gift given to a government official, and in most cases a business leader, should be wrapped in clear plastic so that everyone can see the gift when it is presented.

CHAPTER 5: SOCIAL GRACES

- When a woman enters or leaves a room, all men stand, period. Feminists may be irked by this display of what they feel is chauvinism, but in Mexico it is merely an accepted custom and a display of good manners. If you are a man, stand up. If you are a woman, accept it with grace.

- Who pays for lunch?—the person who extends the invitation. Never wrangle for the check. Dutch treat is a foreign concept; don't try to introduce it.

- Who pays for lunch if the parties include a man and a woman? The rule: a woman *never* pays.

- Nonsmoking areas are virtually unknown in Mexico; if you do not smoke, don't make an issue of it. Remember, when you are outside the U.S., the feelings toward smoking are totally different.

- Being invited to dinner in a Mexican home is a significant sign of acceptance and a personal compliment. Do not refuse, no matter how inconvenient. Prepare for a late dinner and a long, but exceedingly pleasant social interlude.

- Mexicans use their professional designation as a prefix to their name in business introductions (e.g., Licenciado Joaquín Murietta).

- Mexicans have a first name, two last names, and usually a middle name. The first last name is the father's last name and the name you should use in regular dealings or less formal settings.

- A married Mexican woman's second last name, preceded by *de* meaning "of," is her husband's family name and therefore hers as well.

CHAPTER 6: COMMUNICATING

- If you discuss business by telephone or in person, put it on paper and fax it. If your counterpart agrees to the terms, prepare the documents and FedEx them to your contact. Then follow up, follow up, follow up.

- Never assume that an agreement has been reached without a sign-off document.

- Take the time to learn Spanish; the mere fact that you are making the effort will impress your Mexican contacts.

- If you are not fluent, hire a translator for business meetings where technical details are going to be discussed.

- Leave business correspondence to professionals. Draft your letters in English and turn them over to a qualified translator. Have someone fluent in Spanish check the final draft to avoid any embarrassing mistakes.

CHAPTER 7: MAJOR MARKETS

- Primary business and population centers are Mexico City, D.F. (Federal District), Guadalajara, and Monterrey.

- Mexico City is the nation's capital and seat of government as well.

- Monterrey is home base to Mexico's largest industrial conglomerates, Grupo ALFA, Grupo VISA, and Grupo VITRO among others.

- Guadalajara offers a diversity of commerce and industry in an extremely attractive setting.

- The Mexican government is providing incentives to encourage industrial development in other areas of the country.

CHAPTER 8: SETTING UP SHOP

- Direct selling requires constant attention from you or trusted associates. Advantage: Control over your product. Disadvantage: Expense of maintaining staff and merchandise inventory.

- Branch office. Advantage: The opportunity to have U.S.-trained personnel in control of operations. Disadvantages: U.S. employees can only work in Mexico for

183 days during any twelve-month period and the company is subject to taxes at the same level as Mexican companies.

- Broker/representative. Advantage: The representative may already be familiar with your target clientele. Disadvantage: The representative is not exclusively yours.

- Master distributor: requires meticulous attention to detail in developing a working agreement. Advantages: One client to deal with. Ability to ship larger quantities and effect economies. Simplifies recordkeeping. Disadvantages: If master distributor does not perform, you can be out of business before you start. No direct control over marketing techniques. Little or no contact with end-users of your product.

- Joint venture: requires painstaking research to select the right partner. Advantages: An ownership position in your own business in Mexico. Mutual objectives in sales success and profits.

- Hire an attorney well versed in both U.S. and Mexican business law.

- S.A. and S.A. de C.V. are the most frequent addenda to Mexican business names. S.A. stands for Sociedad Anónima—its U.S. counterpart is the famous "Inc."; both mean that the company is a corporation. S.A. de C.V. is a corporation with variable capital.

- All corporations with any degree of foreign ownership must register with and receive authorization from the Ministry of Foreign Affairs and must also register with the National Commission on Foreign Investment.

CHAPTER 9: SHIPPING LOGISTICS

- Shipping into or out of Mexico can be terribly frustrating. Learn the rules, follow the rules, and when that doesn't work hire an expert.

- Ask lots of questions; don't settle for incomplete answers. Get it in writing!

- Don't overlook bonded warehousing. Merchandise can be stored up to five years duty-free and tax deferred.

- Don't overlook foreign trade zone facilities, which offer duty-free holding capability for your merchandise, as well as assembly and repair facilities.

- Know your customs broker!

- Most goods from the U.S. to Mexico or from Mexico to the U.S. go by land transport.

- Any commercial import of $1,000 or more in value must be handled by a Mexican customs house broker.

- Research the different classifications your merchandise can fall under. Select the one with the least duty. Tell your broker how you want your merchandise declared. This can result in substantial savings.

- Insist on a clear estimate of charges prior to shipment, from both the hauler and your customs broker. Prices can vary widely from one shipping period to the next. Get it in writing.

- Follow the guidelines in Factors to Consider when determining how to ship merchandise.

- Review this chapter to learn what brokers are responsible for.

CHAPTER 10: ADVERTISING IN MEXICO

- Mexico media options are as diverse as those in the U.S.

- Hire a U.S. consultant or advertising agency with experience in Mexican media or a firm relationship with a Mexican counterpart.

- Do not try to "do it yourself"; this is a plan for disaster.

- Check the fundamentals. You get what you inspect, not what you expect.

- Conduct field checks for product distribution. If it's not on the shelf, it cannot sell.

- Conduct competitive pricing research.

- If you do not understand Mexico's media units, contracts, and terms, hire someone who does.

- Consider your targeted consumers. Are they part of a large demographic or are they a narrow slice of the market? Select your media accordingly.

CHAPTER 11: THE ART OF GETTING PAID

- Specify payment in U.S. dollars.

- Mexican businesses are usually accustomed to cash transactions. Spell out your requirements on paper and have them approved before you start.

- Keep it simple; get paid in full on the U.S. side for merchandise to be delivered in Mexico.

- If credit is a primary factor in making the deal, select a U.S. bank that deals in international letters of credit. Acquire a confirmed, irrevocable sight letter of credit. The bank is guaranteeing the funds, and the "sight" designation insures that you will receive your money quickly.

- Deal with a banker you know, who knows Mexico and has experience with letters of credit.

CHAPTER 12: ECONOMICS AND THE BANKING SYSTEM

- Banking in Mexico is divided into development banks and commercial banks.

- Development banks are primarily dedicated to the support of government-approved projects.

- Commercial banks are similar to U.S. banks (checking, savings, loans, etc.).

- Bank investments are limited to savings deposits, time deposits, private bank acceptances, and subordinated bank debentures.

- Interest rates are set by individual banks based upon supply and demand. Shop your rates!

CHAPTER 13: THE MEXICAN POLITICAL SYSTEM

- Mexico's president has supreme executive power, without interference from Congress. As the president goes, so goes the Mexican government.

- Read this entire chapter and use the attendant guide to key governmental agencies as you begin to do business in Mexico.

CHAPTER 14: TRAVELING FOR BUSINESS IN MEXICO

- Visitor documents: proof of U.S. citizenship (passport or birth certificate/voter registration card plus photo ID) and Mexican tourist visa.

- Business operators or foreign vendors require U.S. passport and Mexican work permit. Allow at least two weeks to obtain U.S. passport and several weeks to acquire a Mexican work visa from the Mexican embassy or Mexican consulate.

- Driving your car requires a permit. You will need the title and motor vehicle registration from your state to acquire a permit. If driving a company-owned car you will need a notarized affidavit from the company.

- You must have a current driver's license from your state and current license plates.

- Changing money: dollars are widely accepted, but to avoid confusion it is wise to exchange some of your U.S. currency for pesos. Exchanges are located at Mexico City Airport, banks, and money exchange houses (*casas de cambio*).

CHAMBERS OF COMMERCE AND U.S. CONTACTS

If your perception of a chamber of commerce is that of an organization made up of business leaders from various industries mixed with up-and-coming young men and women from a wide variety of enterprises who meet for luncheons and work on committees and exchange business cards, think again. In Mexico, each chamber is specifically dedicated to an industry, business, or service segment.

The largest and most influential of the many chambers are CANACINTRA, the National Chamber of the Manufacturing Industry, with 80,000+ members; CANACO, the Chamber of Commerce of Mexico City, with 50,000+ members (plus its many affiliated chambers throughout the country); and CAINTRA and CAREINTRA, the chambers of industry in Monterrey and Guadalajara, respectively. These last two are effectively the counterparts of CANACINTRA for their regions, but have split off from the main body in order to address their local constituencies.

For your convenience, we have provided a current listing of key chambers of commerce and/or industry in Mexico. If you require an update or access to other business or industry-specific chambers, you may contact CONCAMIN, the organization of chambers of industry, or CONCANACO, the organization of chambers of commerce in Mexico City, which are also listed.

MEXICAN TRADE ASSOCIATIONS/ CHAMBERS OF COMMERCE

American Chamber of Commerce of Mexico, A.C.
Mr. John Bruton
Vice President
Lucerna No. 78
Colonia Juárez
06600 México, D.F.
Tel: (011-52-5) 724-38-00
Fax: (011-52-5) 703-29-11

United States–Mexico Chamber of Commerce
Mr. Martín Rojas
Communications Director
1726 M. Street N.W. Suite 704
Washington, D.C. 20036
Tel: (202) 296-5198
Fax: (202) 728-0768

Cámara Nacional de Comercio de la Ciudad de México (CANACO)
(National Chamber of Commerce of Mexico City)
Lic. Román Vidal Tamayo
Director of Foreign Trade
Paseo de la Reforma No. 42, Piso 3
Colonia Centro
06048 México, D.F.
Tel: (011-52-5) 592-03-75
Fax: (011-52-5) 705-53-10

Confederación de Cámaras Nacionales de Comercio (CON-
CANACO)
(Confederation of National Chambers of Commerce)
Lic. José de Jesús Castellanos López
Director General
Balderas No. 144, Piso 3
Colonia Centro
06079 México, D.F.
Tel: (011-52-5) 709-15-59/709-19-19
Fax: (011-52-5) 709-11-52

Cámara Nacional de la Industria de la Transformación (CANACIN-
TRA)

(National Manufacturing Industry Chamber)
Lic. Luis Miguel Pando Leyva
Director General
Avenida San Antonio No. 256
Colonia Ampliación Nápoles
03849 México, D.F.
Tel: (011-52-5) 563-61-12
Fax: (011-52-5) 598-58-88

Confederación de Cámaras Industriales de los Estados Unidos
Mexicanos (CONCAMIN)
(Confederation of Industrial Chambers of Mexico)
Lic. Alvaro Torres Prieto
Director General
Manuel Ma. Contreras No. 133, Piso 2
Colonia Cuauhtémoc
06500 México, D.F.
Tel: (011-52-5) 566-78-22 Ext. 104/105
Fax: (011-52-5) 535-68-71

Asociación Nacional de Importadores y Exportadores de la
República Mexicana (ANIERM)
(Association of Importers and Exporters of Mexico)
Ing. Juan Autrique Gómez
President
Monterrey No. 130
Colonia Roma 06700
Tel: (011-52-5) 584-95-22
Fax: (011-52-5) 584-53-17

Cámara de la Industria de Transformación de Nuevo León
(CAINTRA)
(Chamber of Industry of Nuevo León)
Ocampo 250 Pte. Cuarto Piso
Monterrey, Nuevo León 64000
Tel: (011-52-83) 45-62-15 and 45-54-40
National Council of Foreign Commerce (CANACEX)
Tlaxcala No. 177 Desp. 803
Colonia Hipódromo
Deleg. Cuauhtémoc
C.P. 06100 México, D.F.
Tel: (011-52-5) 286-87-44 and 286-87-98

Cámara Regional de la Industria de Transformación de Estado
    Jalisco (CAREINTRA)
(Chamber of Industry of Jalisco)
Avenida Washington 1920
Guadalajara, Jalisco 44100
Tel: 611-33-50

Cámara Nacional de Comercio de Jalisco (CANACO)
(National Chamber of Commerce of Jalisco)
Avenida Vallarta 4095
Guadalajara, Jalisco
Tel: 647-80-31

U.S. Government Washington-Based Mexico Contacts

U.S. Department of Commerce
International Trade Administration
Office of NAFTA
Ms. Juliet Bender
Acting Director
14th Street and Constitution Avenue, N.W.
Room No. 3022
Washington, D.C. 20230
Tel: (202) 482-0305
Fax: (202) 482-5865
Flash Fax: (202) 482-4464

Export-Import Bank of the United States
Ms. Marion M. Hinchman
Loan Officer for Mexico
811 Vermont Avenue, N.W.
Washington, D.C. 20571
Tel: (202) 565-3400
Fax: (202) 565-1176

U.S. Trade and Development Agency
Mr. Albert W. Angulo
Program Director
Latin America and the Caribbean
1621 N. Kent Street, Room 309
Rosslyn, VA 22209

Tel: (703) 875-4357
Fax: (703) 875-4009

U.S. Department of State
Bureau of Inter-American Affairs
Office of Mexican Affairs
Mr. Dennis Heys
Director
21st and C Streets, N.W., Room 4258
Washington, D.C. 20520
Tel: (202) 647-9894
Fax: (202) 647-5752

Office of the United States Trade Representative
Mr. John Melle
Director of Mexican Affairs
600 17th Street, N.W.
Washington, D.C. 20006
Tel: (202) 395-3412
Fax: (202) 395-3911

TRADE COMMISSION OF MEXICO IN THE U.S./MEXICAN INVESTMENT BOARD

Embassy of Mexico
1911 Pennsylvania Ave, N.W.
Washington, D.C. 20006
Tel: (202) 728-1600
Fax: (202) 728-1793

Mexican Investment Board
Tel: 011 (525) 202-7804
Fax: 011 (525) 202-7925

The MIB has asked U.S. corporations requesting investment info on Mexico to fax a brief description of their current business activities, their expansion plans in Mexico, and other pertinent info regarding their product, sales and distribution structure, and company history to the MIB. The MIB requests that U.S. companies fax this info prior to telephoning the Mexico City MIB office.

The Trade Commission of Mexico is the country's primary export promotion agency. It maintains the following offices in the United States to assist those interested in importing from Mexico:

California
350 South Figueroa Street
World Trade Center Suite 296
Los Angeles, CA 90071
Tel: (213) 628-1220
Fax: (213) 628-8466

Florida
100 N. Biscayne Blvd.
Suite 1601
Miami, FL 33132
Tel: (305) 372-9929
Fax: (305) 374-1238

Georgia
229 Peachtree Street, N.E.
Suite 917 Cain Tower Bldg.
Atlanta, GA 30343
Tel: (404) 522-5373
Fax: (404) 681-3361

Illinois
Illinois Center
225 North Michigan Avenue
Suite 1800

Chicago, IL 60601
Tel: (312) 856-0316
Fax: (312) 856-1834

New York
375 Park Avenue
19th Floor
Suite 1905
New York, NY 10152
Tel: (212) 826-2916
Fax: (212) 826-2979

Texas (Dallas)
2777 Stemmons Frwy.
Suite 1622
Dallas, TX 75207
Tel: (214) 688-4096
Fax: (214) 905-3831

Texas (San Antonio)
1100 N.W. Loop 410
Suite 409
San Antonio, TX 73213
Tel: (210) 525-9748
Fax: (210) 525-8355

U.S. EMBASSY/CONSULATE TRADE PERSONNEL

U.S. Embassy, Mexico City
Mr. Kevin C. Brennan
Minister-Counselor
Mr. John Harris
Commercial Counselor
Paseo de la Reforma No. 305
Colonia Cuauhtémoc
06500 México, D.F.
Tel: (011-52-5) 211-00-42,
    Ext. 3730
Fax: (011-52-5) 207-89-38
Mail: P.O. Box No. 3087
Laredo, TX 78044-3087

U.S. Trade Center, Mexico City
Mr. Robert W. Miller
Director
Liverpool No. 31
Colonia Juárez
06600 México, D.F.
Tel: (011-52-5) 591-01-55
Fax: (011-52-5) 566-11-15
Mail: P.O. Box No. 3087
Laredo, TX 78044-3087

U.S. Agricultural Trade Office
Mr. Marvin Lehrer
Director
Edificio Virreyes, PH-2
Monte Pelvoux No. 220
Lomas de Chapultepec
11000 México, D.F.
Tel: (011-52-5) 202-04-34
Fax: (011-52-5) 202-05-28
Mail: P.O. Box No. 3087
Laredo, TX 78044-3087

U.S. Consulate General,
Monterrey
Mr. Robert Jones
Commercial Officer
Avenida Constitución
No. 411 Pte.

64000 Monterrey, NL
Tel: (011-52-83) 45-21-20
Fax: (011-52-83) 42-51-72
Mail: P.O. Box No. 3098
Laredo, TX 78044-3098

U.S. Consulate, Guadalajara
Mr. Bryan Smith
Commercial Officer
Progreso No. 175
44100 Guadalajara, Jalisco
Tel: (011-52-3) 625-29-98
Fax: (011-52-3) 625-35-76
Mail: P.O. Box No. 3088
Laredo, TX 78044-3088

OTHER WASHINGTON-BASED U.S. GOVERNMENT DEPARTMENTS WITH MEXICO DESKS

Agency	Office Telephone
Department of Agriculture	Mexico Desk (202) 720-1340
Department of Defense	Mexico Desk (703) 697-9301
Department of Energy	Mexico Desk (202) 586-5906
Environmental Protection Agency	Mexico Desk (202) 260-4890
Department of Interior	Mexico Desk (202) 501-9688
Department of Labor	NAFTA (202) 501-6653
Department of Labor (fax line)	NAFTA (202) 273-3454
Overseas Private Investment Corporation	Latin America (202) 336-8492
Department of Transportation	Mexico Desk (202) 366-2892
Department of Treasury	Trade-Mexico (202) 622-1539
	Mexico Desk (202) 622-1276
	Invest-Mexico (202) 622-1860
U.S. Information Agency	Mexico Desk (202) 619-6835

NAME PROTOCOL

Here's a listing of sample names as you might see them on business cards, correspondence, etc.: (T) = title (F) = first name (M) = middle name (L) = last name (Mat) = maternal last name (MdN) = maiden name

Mario(F) Alberto(M) Martínez(L) Sánchez(Mat)
Address as:
Mario Martínez or Sr. Martínez

Lic.(T) Santiago(F) Rodríguez(L) de la Rosa(Mat)
Address as:
Santiago Rodríguez or Lic. Rodríguez

Arq.(T) Luis(F) Santos(L) C.(Mat)
Address as:
Luis Santos or Arq. Santos

María(F) Lourdes(M) García(L) Hernández(Mat)
Address as:
María García or Srta. García

Estela(F) Sánchez(MdN) de Chávez(L)
Address as:
Estela Chávez or Sra. Chávez

Lic.(T) Rosa(F) Méndez(L) Garza(Mat)
Address as:
Rosa Méndez or Lic. Méndez

Lic.(T) Miguel(F) de la Madrid(L) Hurtado(Mat)
Address as:
Miguel de la Madrid or Lic. de la Madrid

Lic.(T) Carlos(F) Salinas(L) de Gortari(Mat)
Address as:
Carlos Salinas—always Sr. Presidente

HOLIDAYS

Just as in the U.S. and every other country, Mexico recognizes certain historic events and traditions, as well as the presidential election, by declaring holidays.

Of particular interest to business are two significant holiday periods that occur within the school year: the two-week period for Christmas and New Year's and the two weeks prior to Easter. These are both important holidays, and many business people travel with their families during these periods.

Based upon our own experiences, we advise you to note all of these holidays on your business calendar and check with your Mexican contacts before planning meetings or shipments to or from Mexico.

We learned from experience, and it was an expensive course.

IMPORTANT MEXICAN HOLIDAYS

New Year's Day	January 1
Constitution Day	February 5
Benito Juárez' Birthday	March 21
Easter Observance (Semana Santa)	10 days prior to Easter Sunday
Labor Day	May 1
Cinco de Mayo	May 5

Mother's Day	May 10 (half day)
Presidential Elections	July 6 (every six years)
Independence Anniversary	September 16
All Saints' Day	November 1
Anniversary of Mexican Revolution	November 20
Change of Fed. Executive Power	December 1 (every six years)
Christmas	December 25

MEXICAN CONSULATES IN NORTH AMERICA

You may obtain tourist and/or work visas at these consulates.

CANADA

Montreal
2000 Mansfield Street, Suite
   1015
Montreal, Quebec 113A 2Z7

Toronto
60 Bloor Street West, Suite 203
Toronto, Ontario M4W 3B8
Tel: (416) 922-2718/922-3196

Vancouver
810-1130 West Pender
Vancouver, British Columbia
   VGE 4A4
Tel: (604) 684-3547/684-1859
Fax: (604) 684-2485

U.S.A.

Albuquerque
401 5th Street N.W.
Western Bank Bldg.
Albuquerque, NM 87102
Tel: (505) 247-2147/247-2139

Atlanta
410 South Tower One CNN
   Center
Atlanta, GA 30303
Tel: (404) 688-3258/688-3261

Austin
200 East 6th Street, Suite 200
Hanning Row Building
Austin, TX 78701
Tel: (512) 478-2866/478-9031

Boston
20 Park Plaza—Suite 1212
Boston, MA 02116
Tel: (617) 426-4942/426-8782
Fax: (617) 426-5795

Brownsville
Elizabeth and East 7th
Brownsville, TX 78520
Tel: (512) 542-2051/542-4431

Calexico
331 West Second Street
Calexico, CA 92231
Tel: (619) 357-3863/357-3880

Chicago
300 North Michigan Avenue
Chicago, IL 60601
Tel: (312) 855-1380/855-1367

Corpus Christi
800 North Shore Line Blvd
One Shoreline Plaza,
    410 North Tower
Corpus Christi, TX 78401
Tel: (512) 882-3375/882-5964
Fax: (512) 882-9324

Dallas
1349 Empire Central, Suite 100
Dallas, TX 75247
Tel: (214) 630-7341/630-2024

Del Rio
1010 South Main Street
Del Rio, TX 78841
Tel: (512) 775-2352/774-5031
Fax: (512) 775-9451

Denver
707 Washington Street, Suite A
Denver, CO 80203
Tel: (303) 830-0607/830-0601
Fax: (303) 830-0704

Detroit
1249 Washington Blvd, Suite
    1513
Book Bldg.

Detroit, MI 48226
Tel: (313) 965-1868/965-1869

Eagle Pass
140 Adams Street
Eagle Pass, TX 78832
Tel: (512) 773-9255/773-9263

El Paso
910 East San Antonio Street
El Paso, TX 79901
Tel: (915) 533-3634/533-3645
Fax: (915) 532-7153

Fresno
905 N. Fulton Street
Fresno, CA 93728
Tel: (209) 233-3065/233-9770
Fax: (209) 233-5638

Houston
4200 Montrose Blvd, Suite 120
Houston, TX 77006
Tel: (713) 524-2300/524-4861

Laredo
1612 Farragut Street
Laredo, TX 78040
Tel: (512) 723-0990/723-6360
Fax: (512) 723-1741

Los Angeles
2401 West 6th Street
Los Angeles, CA 90057
Tel: (213) 351-6800/361-6010
Fax: (213) 398-9186

McAllen
1418 Beech Street, Suites 102
    & 104
McAllen, TX 78501
Tel: (512) 682-0243/686-0253
Fax: (512) 686-4901

Miami
780 N.W. Le Jeune Road, Suite 525
Miami, FL 33126
Tel: (305) 441-8780/441-6523
Fax: (305) 441-7180

Midland
511 W. Ohio, Suite 121
Midland, TX 79701
Tel: (915) 687-2334/687-2335

New Orleans
1140 World Trade Center Bldg.
2 Canal Street
New Orleans, LA 70130
Tel: (504) 522-3596/522-3597

New York
8 East 41st Street
New York, NY 10017
Tel: (212) 689-0456/689-0460
Fax: (212) 545-8197

Nogales
135 Terrace Avenue
Nogales, AZ 85021
Tel: (602) 287-2521/287-4850

Oxnard
Oxnard Transportation Center
Oxnard, CA 93030
Tel: (805) 483-8066/483-4684

Philadelphia
575 Bourse Bldg.; 21 S. 5th St.
Philadelphia, PA 19106
Tel: (215) 922-4262/922-3834
Fax: (215) 923-7281

Phoenix
1990 West Camelback, Suite 110
Phoenix, AZ 85015

Tel: (602) 242-7398
Fax: (602) 242-2957

Sacramento
9800 Old Winerg Place
Sacramento, CA 95827
Tel: (916) 446-4696/446-9024

St. Louis
1015 Locust Street, Suite 922
St. Louis, MO 63101
Tel: (314) 436-3233/436-3426

Salt Lake City
182 South 600 East, Suite 202
Salt Lake City, UT 84102
Tel: (801) 521-8502/521-8503

San Antonio
127 Navarro Street
San Antonio, TX 78205
Tel: (210) 227-9145/227-9728
Fax: (210) 227-1817

San Bernardino
588 West 6th Street
San Bernardino, CA 92401
Tel: (714) 888-2500/888-4700

San Diego
610 "A" 1st Floor
1549 India Street
San Diego, CA 92101
Tel: (619) 231-8414
Fax: (619) 392-3233

San Francisco
870 Market Street, Suite 528
San Francisco, CA 94102
Tel: (415) 392-5554/392-6576

San Jose
380 North First Street, Suite 102

San Jose, CA 95112
Tel: (408) 294-3415
Fax: (408) 294-4506

Santa Ana
406 West 4th Street
Santa Ana, CA 92701
Tel: (714) 835-3749/835-3069

Seattle
2132 Third Avenue
Seattle, WA 98121
Tel: (206) 448-6819/448-8435
Fax: (206) 448-4771

Tucson
553 S. Stone Avenue
Tucson, AZ 85701
Tel: (602) 882-5595/882-5596

DIALING CODES
FOR MEXICAN CITIES

To dial Mexico from the U.S. or Canada, dial 011-52 + a city code from the following list + the local number. (Note: if you don't find the city as "X," look under "Cd. X.")

Abasolo, Gto. 469
Acámbaro, Gto. 447
Acambay, Méx. 722
Acaponeta, Nay. 325
Acapulco, Gro. 74
Acatic, Jal. 371
Acatlán, Pue. 953
Acatlán de Juárez, Jal. 377
Acatlán de Pérez, Oax. 274
Acatlipa, Mor. 739
Acatzingo, Pue. 242
Acayucán, Ver. 924
Acero, Coah. 863
Actopan, Hgo. 772
Aculco, Méx. 722
Adolfo Ruiz Cortines, Sin. 689
Agua Dulce, Ver. 923
Agua Prieta, Son. 633
Agualeguas, N.L. 899

Aguascalientes, Ags. 49
Aguililla, Mich. 453
Agujita, Coah. 861
Ahome, Sin. 686
Ahuacatlán, Nay. 324
Ahualulco, Jal. 375
Ajalpan, Pue. 238
Ajijíc, Jal. 376
Alamo Temapache, Ver. 784
Alamos, Son. 642
Alazán, Ver. 785
Almoloya de Juárez, Méx. 723
Altamira, Tamps. 126
Altar, Son. 637
Altepexi, Pue. 238
Altotonga, Ver. 231
Alvarado, Ver. 297
Allende, N.L. 826
Allenoe, Coah. 862

Cotija de la Paz, Mich. 353
Coyuca de Benítez, Gro. 745
Cozumel, Q.R. 987
Creel, Chih. 145
Cruz Azul, Hgo. 778
Cuajimalpa, D.F. 5
Cuajinicuilapa, Gro. 741
Cuatro Ciénegas, Coah. 869
Cuauhtémoc, Col. 332
Cuautitlán, Méx. 5
Cuautla, Mor. 735
Cuencamé, Dgo. 176
Cuerámaro, Gto. 462
Cuernavaca, Mor. 73
Cuetzalán, Pue. 233
Cuicatlán, Oax. 237
Cuitláhuac, Ver. 273
Culiacán, Sin. 67
Cunduacán, Tab. 933
Cutzamala de Pinzón, Gro. 767
Chacaltianguis, Ver. 288
Chahuites, Oax. 971
Chalco, Méx. 597
Champotón, Camp. 981
Chapala, Jal. 376
Charcas, S.L.P. 485
Chavinda, Mich. 354
Chetumal, Q.R. 983
Chiapa de Corzo, Chis. 961
Chiconcuac, Méx. 595
Chicontepec, Ver. 125
Chignahuapán, Pue. 777
Chihuahua, Chih. 14
Chilapa, Gro. 747
Chilchota, Mich. 351
Chimalhuacán, Méx. 595
Chimalpa, Méx. 597
China, N.L. 823
Chipancingo, Gro. 747
Chipilo, Pue. 22

Cholula, Pue. 22
Degollado, Jal. 352
Dr. Arroyo, N.L. 488
Dr. Porfirio Parra, Chih. 166
Dolores Hidalgo, Gto. 468
Dos Ríos, Méx. 728
Durango, Dgo. 181
Dzitbalché, Camp. 996
Ebano, S.L.P. 126
El Alamo, N.L. 828
El Carmen, N.L. 823
El Coyote, Coah. 177
El Dorado, Sin. 672
El Fuerte, Sin. 689
El Grullo, Jal. 338
El Higo, Ver. 126
El Molinco, Chih. 157
El Oro, Méx. 722
El Porvenir, Chih. 166
El Realito, Tamps. 894
El Salto, Dgo. 187
El Salto, Jal. 373
El Terrero, Chih. 157
El Triunto, Tab. 934
Emiliano Zapata, Hgo. 596
Emiliano Zapata, Méx. 597
Emiliano Zapata, Tab. 934
Emilio Carranza, Ver. 232
Empalme, Son. 622
Encarnación de Díaz, Jal. 495
Ensenada, B.C. 617
Etchojoa, Son. 642
Etzatlán, Jal. 375
Excuinapa, Sin. 695
Felipe Carrillo Puerto, Mich.
    457
Felipe Carrillo Puerto, Q.R. 983
Fortín, Ver. 271
Fracc. Las Delicias, Méx. 597
Framboyanes, Ver. 29

CURRENCY CONVERSION CHARTS

TABLE 2. QUICK REFERENCE CURRENCY CONVERSION
DOLLARS TO NEW PESOS

Exchange Rate	1 Peso Equals	$1.00	$5.00	$10.00	$20.00	$50.00	$100
6.0	$.1667	N$6.00	N$30.00	N$60.00	N$120.00	N$300.00	N$600.00
6.1	$.1639	N$6.10	N$30.50	N$61.00	N$122.00	N$305.00	N$610.00
6.2	$.1613	N$6.20	N$31.00	N$62.00	N$124.00	N$310.00	N$620.00
6.3	$.1587	N$6.30	N$31.50	N$63.00	N$126.00	N$315.00	N$630.00
6.4	$.1563	N$6.40	N$32.00	N$64.00	N$128.00	N$320.00	N$640.00
6.5	$.1538	N$6.50	N$32.50	N$65.00	N$130.00	N$325.00	N$650.00
6.6	$.1515	N$6.60	N$33.00	N$66.00	N$132.00	N$330.00	N$660.00
6.7	$.1493	N$6.70	N$33.50	N$67.00	N$134.00	N$335.00	N$670.00
6.8	$.1471	N$6.80	N$34.00	N$68.00	N$136.00	N$340.00	N$680.00
6.9	$.1449	N$6.90	N$34.50	N$69.00	N$138.00	N$345.00	N$690.00
7.0	$.1429	N$7.00	N$35.00	N$70.00	N$140.00	N$350.00	N$700.00
7.1	$.1408	N$7.10	N$35.50	N$71.00	N$142.00	N$355.00	N$710.00
7.2	$.1389	N$7.20	N$36.00	N$72.00	N$144.00	N$360.00	N$720.00
7.3	$.1370	N$7.30	N$36.50	N$73.00	N$146.00	N$365.00	N$730.00
7.4	$.1351	N$7.40	N$37.00	N$74.00	N$148.00	N$370.00	N$740.00
7.5	$.1333	N$7.50	N$37.50	N$75.00	N$150.00	N$375.00	N$750.00
7.6	$.1316	N$7.60	N$38.00	N$76.00	N$152.00	N$380.00	N$760.00
7.7	$.1299	N$7.70	N$38.50	N$77.00	N$154.00	N$385.00	N$770.00

7.8	$.1282	N$7.80	N$39.00	N$78.00	N$156.00	N$390.00	N$780.00
7.9	$.1266	N$7.90	N$39.50	N$79.00	N$158.00	N$395.00	N$790.00
8.0	$.1250	N$8.00	N$40.00	N$80.00	N$160.00	N$400.00	N$800.00
8.1	$.1235	N$8.10	N$40.50	N$81.00	N$162.00	N$405.00	N$810.00
8.2	$.1220	N$8.20	N$41.00	N$82.00	N$164.00	N$410.00	N$820.00
8.3	$.1205	N$8.30	N$41.50	N$83.00	N$166.00	N$415.00	N$830.00
8.4	$.1190	N$8.40	N$42.00	N$84.00	N$168.00	N$420.00	N$840.00
8.5	$.1176	N$8.50	N$42.50	N$85.00	N$170.00	N$425.00	N$850.00
8.6	$.1163	N$8.60	N$43.00	N$86.00	N$172.00	N$430.00	N$860.00
8.7	$.1149	N$8.70	N$43.50	N$87.00	N$174.00	N$435.00	N$870.00
8.8	$.1136	N$8.80	N$44.00	N$88.00	N$176.00	N$440.00	N$880.00
8.9	$.1124	N$8.90	N$44.50	N$89.00	N$178.00	N$445.00	N$890.00
9.0	$.1111	N$9.00	N$45.00	N$90.00	N$180.00	N$450.00	N$900.00
9.1	$.1099	N$9.10	N$45.50	N$91.00	N$182.00	N$455.00	N$910.00
9.2	$.1087	N$9.20	N$46.00	N$92.00	N$184.00	N$460.00	N$920.00
9.3	$.1075	N$9.30	N$46.50	N$93.00	N$186.00	N$465.00	N$930.00
9.4	$.1064	N$9.40	N$47.00	N$94.00	N$188.00	N$470.00	N$940.00
9.5	$.1053	N$9.50	N$47.50	N$95.00	N$190.00	N$475.00	N$950.00
9.6	$.1042	N$9.60	N$48.00	N$96.00	N$192.00	N$480.00	N$960.00
9.7	$.1031	N$9.70	N$48.50	N$97.00	N$194.00	N$485.00	N$970.00
9.8	$.1020	N$9.80	N$49.00	N$98.00	N$196.00	N$490.00	N$980.00
10.0	$.1000	N$10.00	N$50.00	N$100.00	N$200.00	N$500.00	N$1000.00

TABLE 3. QUICK REFERENCE CURRENCY CONVERSION
NEW PESOS TO DOLLARS

Exchange Rate	N$1.00	N$2.00	N$5.00	N$10.00	N$20.00	N$50.00	N$100	N$200
6.0	$0.17	$0.33	$0.83	$1.67	$3.33	$8.33	$16.67	$33.33
6.1	$0.16	$0.33	$0.82	$1.64	$3.28	$8.20	$16.39	$32.79
6.2	$0.16	$0.32	$0.81	$1.61	$3.23	$8.06	$16.13	$32.26
6.3	$0.16	$0.32	$0.79	$1.59	$3.17	$7.94	$15.87	$31.75
6.4	$0.16	$0.31	$0.78	$1.56	$3.13	$7.81	$15.63	$31.25
6.5	$0.15	$0.31	$0.77	$1.54	$3.08	$7.69	$15.38	$30.77
6.6	$0.15	$0.30	$0.76	$1.52	$3.03	$7.58	$15.15	$30.30
6.7	$0.15	$0.30	$0.75	$1.49	$2.99	$7.46	$14.93	$29.85
6.8	$0.15	$0.29	$0.74	$1.47	$2.94	$7.35	$14.71	$29.41
6.9	$0.14	$0.29	$0.72	$1.45	$2.90	$7.25	$14.49	$28.99
7.0	$0.14	$0.29	$0.71	$1.43	$2.86	$7.14	$14.29	$28.57
7.1	$0.14	$0.28	$0.70	$1.41	$2.82	$7.04	$14.08	$28.17
7.2	$0.14	$0.28	$0.69	$1.39	$2.78	$6.94	$13.89	$27.78
7.3	$0.14	$0.27	$0.68	$1.37	$2.74	$6.85	$13.70	$27.40
7.4	$0.14	$0.27	$0.68	$1.35	$2.70	$6.76	$13.51	$27.03
7.5	$0.13	$0.27	$0.67	$1.33	$2.67	$6.67	$13.33	$26.67
7.6	$0.13	$0.26	$0.66	$1.32	$2.63	$6.58	$13.16	$26.32
7.7	$0.13	$0.26	$0.65	$1.30	$2.60	$6.49	$12.99	$25.97

7.8	$0.13	$0.26	$0.64	$1.28	$2.56	$6.41	$12.82	$25.64
7.9	$0.13	$0.25	$0.63	$1.27	$2.53	$6.33	$12.66	$25.32
8.0	$0.13	$0.25	$0.63	$1.25	$2.50	$6.25	$12.50	$25.00
8.1	$0.12	$0.25	$0.62	$1.23	$2.47	$6.17	$12.35	$24.69
8.2	$0.12	$0.24	$0.61	$1.22	$2.44	$6.10	$12.20	$24.39
8.3	$0.12	$0.24	$0.60	$1.20	$2.41	$6.02	$12.05	$24.10
8.4	$0.12	$0.24	$0.60	$1.19	$2.38	$5.95	$11.90	$23.81
8.5	$0.12	$0.24	$0.59	$1.18	$2.35	$5.88	$11.76	$23.53
8.6	$0.12	$0.23	$0.58	$1.16	$2.33	$5.81	$11.63	$23.26
8.7	$0.11	$0.23	$0.57	$1.15	$2.30	$5.75	$11.49	$22.99
8.8	$0.11	$0.23	$0.57	$1.14	$2.27	$5.68	$11.36	$22.73
8.9	$0.11	$0.22	$0.56	$1.12	$2.25	$5.62	$11.24	$22.47
9.0	$0.11	$0.22	$0.56	$1.11	$2.22	$5.56	$11.11	$22.22
9.1	$0.11	$0.22	$0.55	$1.10	$2.20	$5.49	$10.99	$21.98
9.2	$0.11	$0.22	$0.54	$1.09	$2.17	$5.43	$10.87	$21.74
9.3	$0.11	$0.22	$0.54	$1.08	$2.15	$5.38	$10.75	$21.51
9.4	$0.11	$0.21	$0.53	$1.06	$2.13	$5.32	$10.64	$21.28
9.5	$0.11	$0.21	$0.53	$1.05	$2.11	$5.26	$10.53	$21.05
9.6	$0.10	$0.21	$0.52	$1.04	$2.08	$5.21	$10.42	$20.83
9.7	$0.10	$0.21	$0.52	$1.03	$2.06	$5.15	$10.31	$20.62
9.8	$0.10	$0.20	$0.51	$1.02	$2.04	$5.10	$10.20	$20.41
10.0	$0.10	$0.20	$0.50	$1.00	$2.00	$5.00	$10.00	$20.00

CONVERSION TABLES FOR U.S. AND METRIC MEASUREMENTS

Mexico and nearly the entire rest of the world is on the metric system. International business requires you to have metric fluency. It's easy to substitute meters for yards, think of approximately two pounds per kilogram, three kilometers to every two miles, liter for quart, 30 grams an ounce, etc.

LINEAR
1 in = 2.54 cm	1 mm = .03937 in
1 ft = 30.48 cm	1 cm = .3937 in
1 yd = .914 mts	1 mt 3.28 ft = 1.09 yds
1 mi = 1.61 km	1 km = .621 mi

WEIGHT
1 oz = 28.3495 gm	1 gm = .035 oz
1 lb = .4536 kg	1 kg = 2.204 lbs
1 ton = 907.18 kg	1 M.T. = 1.1 tons

COOKING:
1 tbsp = 15 ml	1 tsp = 5 ml
1/2 tsp = 2.5 ml	1/4 tsp = 1.25 ml

AREA
1 sq in. = 6.451 sq cm	1 sq cm = .155 sq in
1 sq ft = .0929 sq mts	1 sq mt = 10.763 sq ft
1 sq yd = .836 sq mts	1 sq mt = 1.195 sq yd
1 acre = .4047 hectares	1 hectare = 2.47 acres

VOLUME
1 oz = 29.58 ml	1 ml = .0348 oz
1 qt = .946 l	1 l = 1.057 qt
1 gal = 3.785 l	1 l = .264 gal
1 cu in = 16.39 cu cm	1 cu cm = .061 cu in
1 cu ft = .028 cu mts	1 cu mt = 35.315 cu ft
1 cu yd = .765 cu mts	1 cu mt = 1.308 cu yd

TEMPERATURE:
To convert Celsius into Fahrenheit multiply Celsius degrees by 9, divide by 5, add 32. From Fahrenheit into Celsius subtract 32 from degrees of Fahrenheit, multiply by 5, then divide by 9.

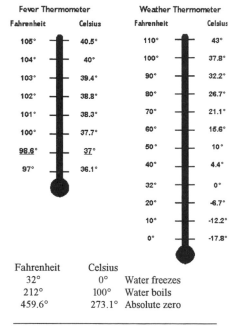

Fever Thermometer		Weather Thermometer	
Fahrenheit	Celsius	Fahrenheit	Celsius
105°	40.5°	110°	43°
104°	40°	100°	37.8°
103°	39.4°	90°	32.2°
102°	38.8°	80°	26.7°
101°	38.3°	70°	21.1°
100°	37.7°	60°	15.6°
98.6°	37°	50°	10°
97°	36.1°	40°	4.4°
		32°	0°
		20°	-6.7°
		10°	-12.2°
		0°	-17.8°

Fahrenheit	Celsius	
32°	0°	Water freezes
212°	100°	Water boils
459.6°	273.1°	Absolute zero

Speedometer Conversion

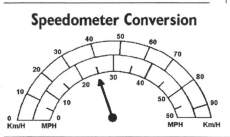

Abbreviations:

inch/in, foot/ft, yard/yd, mile/mi, ounce/oz, pound/lb, quart/qt, gallon/gal, tablespoon/tbsp, teaspoon/tsp

millimeter/mm, centimeter/cm, meter/mt, kilometer/km, gram/gm, kilogram/kg, milliliter/ml, liter/l, metric ton/M.T.

INDEX